Animal

Self Help Revelations from The Animal Kingdom

By Jane Giddings BACP

All Feedback Appreciated at

ask@animalreflections.co.uk

www.animalreflections.co.uk

"This really is a beautiful read. It is a unique book and there is nothing else quite like it. It is a gorgeous book about animals and their meanings, but it's also a really positive, inspirational and innovative self help book. I thoroughly enjoyed it from start to finish. :) Laura (Amazon Reviewer)

"Only read a bit of it so far, but very interesting psychological input of the meanings of animals represented in life. The hamster (going around in circles over and over) and the rabbit (scared) reminds me of my pets when I was younger , my power animals - both represent my life right now, to know what it all means helps you to understand and be aware of signs of animals around you, to make better decisions and feel better in yourself! (Amazon Reviewer)

"Was very curious to read this book as there have been a couple of animals disturbing me of late, this really helped me figure out what was going on in my life and how to put things right, can't thank you enough for giving me such clarity, fantastic self help book, well done for this!! Brilliant Jojo (Amazon Reviewer)

"I just wanted to write to tell you how inspiring and uplifting I found your book. The meanings and symbols connect and resonate with me on so many levels. I particularly, loved your chapter on feathers ! A brilliant read that I know I will dip into throughout my life.
Thank you for the insights - with love, Laura (Amazon)

"Brilliant. The book is entertaining and very enjoyable to read. Very informative about how the animal kingdom gives us messages we never knew about. Great for quick references and self help. Can't wait to read the meaning of the bee. Thoroughly recommend it. (Amazon Reviewer)

"I give 5 stars for this book a truly fascinating book which opens the eyes about the animal kingdom and revelations and deeper meanings I very much my c h recommend this book you won't put it down from start to finish" (Amazon)

"Informative and simplistic, easy to read and thought provoking questions make this an essential self help guide on my personal and spiritual journey. I shall be refering back to this book forever" Donna (Amazon Reviewer)

"Such an inspirational book around animal and life meanings.very beautifully written ,enjoyed it from start to finish" (Amazon Reviewer)

"A wonderful read, inspirational and applicable to so many situations I'm life. A must read....thank you Jane this book has changed my approach and view I'm so many things in life.... (Amazon Reviewer)

"I am only 16, and read a little bit of the book and so far I love it, it is a truly inspirational book, and I hope to read more of this book, I recommend it to any one to read it" Chloe (Amazon Reviewer)

"I have known Jane for almost 20 years, she really is a true inspiration to all! Animal reflections is really going to help to guide myself and all who reads it. It's amazing to know just how much we can learn from the animal kingdom" Nicola (Amazon Reviewer)

"Reading this book made me really think, sometimes these animals do appear when going through different emotions. Well written, good and interesting read" (Amazon Reviewer)

Preface

It's not by chance that you're reading this introduction. This book has chosen **YOU**!!! For you have been divinely guided at this right time of your life to understand this books important messages, just for **YOU**!!!

This self help book is like no other. It is unique in the way that it links messages from the Animal Kingdom to your conscious mind. Improving our connection and awareness to what is really going on in our everyday life.

This is a not a book to just read once and forget about. It's a quick and easy reference guide that you can use every day.

Daily usage of this personal growth book will provide you with the insight, knowledge, wisdom and humour for your everyday survival. So you may learn to overcome daily disappointments, setbacks and obstacles.

Animal Reflections helps you to become tolerant and accepting of others. The information contained will encourage you to become who you truly are, to realise we're not separate and on this journey of life on our own. **We are all connected and here to help and support one another.**

Every creature has its own message that can be positive and inspiring or a warning of a challenge or an obstacle that possibly is heading your way.

Animal Reflections will help you to become a more thoughtful, caring and understanding person, with a greater self-awareness and balance in your daily life.

This self-help book will not only support and guide you but it will change the way you think and act towards the Animal Kingdom.

You will be truly inspired, amazed and uplifted at the way these creatures live their everyday life to help and guide us when we really need it.

Through the Law of Attraction, I will teach you how to understand and interpret the Animal Kingdom's strong presence, personal messages and behaviour. Thereby opening up your mind to the endless opportunities for help, support and spiritual growth. Because as humans we have disconnected from the elements of nature and lost our way.

If you are going through a difficult time in your life this book will give you a different perspective, approach and outlook on life.

Animal Reflections encourages you stop being a victim and replace hidden negative patterns of behaviour that you may or may not be aware of.

You will then be encouraged to take responsibility for your own behaviour and actions, **training you to become your own therapist**, promoting self-awareness and self-reliance.

The time is **NOW!**

Are you up for the challenge, ready for change and **ACTION**?

About the Author

Jane Giddings is a full time therapist who runs a teaching and healing school in the West of England.

The information contained within this book is based on her 25 Years of experience as a qualified Fellow member of the Federation of Holistic Therapists (FFHT). A senior Hypnotherapist on the General Hypnotherapy Register (GHR). A Psychotherapist, Counsellor and Supervisor registered with the British Association for Counselling & Psychotherapy (BACP).

Jane Giddings is also a member of the Complimentary Therapists Association (CTHA) Registered with the Complimentary & Natural Health Care Council (CNHC). Supervisor & accredited member of the National Counselling Society (NCS). A Senior Accreditation & member of the National Council of Psychotherapists (NCP).

Besides the above, Jane has worked for two years in a secure unit and eight years with young offenders within Her Majesty's Prison Service.

Jane has supported, numerous schools and youth clubs within the United Kingdom.

For the last five years, Jane has worked as a Barnardos Adoption Agency Counsellor.

Important Note from the Author

Even though Jane Giddings is a highly qualified therapist, she is not a medical professional.

The information presented in this book is educational in nature and is provided only as general information. Therefore, the author strongly advises that you seek professional medical advice as appropriate, before making any health decisions.

The author accepts no responsibility or liability whatsoever for the use or misuse of the information contained in this book.

The revelations contained within this book, have been specifically and deliberately written in a clear and occasionally humorous way. So its important messages will reach those aged 7 to 100!

Acknowledgements

Millions of sincere thanks, love and appreciation to Nick Hall my beautiful technical co-creator who patiently and painstakingly sat with me for hours and hours, putting this book together. Without Nick's support there wouldn't have been a book, so I'll always be eternally grateful to him.

Much love and appreciation to my lovely daughters Laura & Hollie and my adorable grandchildren. Thank you for always being there for me.

Many thanks to all my lovely friends and clients for requesting their animal messages in the last 20 years.

A huge thank you to Bev for helping me get to where I am today.

And finally this book is specially dedicated to the following:

Albert the Peacock, Charlie the Cat,

Flur the Rabbit, Eddie the Bird,

Barney, Ruby and Toby the Dogs.

Thank you all for the lessons you've taught me and the love we've shared.

How to Use This Book

To get the best information from this book, if you have spotted, seen or heard your Animal, go ahead and look it up in the book. There might be one message or numerous messages from that Animal that may resonate with you.

Animals can appear in the sky, as a shape in the clouds, when you're out walking in nature, in a dream, on the television, in a book or magazine, on a billboard, or when you're out shopping. You may hear the animal's name mentioned on the radio, in a song, or in a conversation.

If you are blocked or feel you haven't seen an animal, there is still a message for you. Close your eyes and point or tap the animal index of this book and on the page that has been selected there could be an important message just for you.

Over 25 years of experience, the powerful information in this book, is based upon my personal discoveries through client sessions of a creature or animal, that I had seen or thought of before the beginning of the session.

For example,

If I saw a worm, I would know the client was stuck and kept going over the same patterns of behaviour in life.

Before I became a qualified therapist, I kept seeing caterpillars and butterflies when I was personally going through a tough, painful and ugly time in my life. As I look back now I realise the very powerful hidden meaning of the caterpillar every time I was feeling down, in pain, life was ugly and I felt insignificant.

The sight of the caterpillar was reflecting back my thoughts and behaviour (Which I was totally unaware of then).

I used to look at the caterpillar and think I know how you feel mate! (Little did I know the true meaning, which still amazes me now).

Its message is a holistic approach, starting at the root cause, addressing the pain and dealing with any issues. Although uncomfortable and painful to work through, metamorphosis was taking place.

This was opening the pathway to transformation, healing and freedom, (turning in to the light hearted butterfly). I then trained and qualified as a Psychotherapist, Hypnotherapist, Counsellor and working with people from all walks of life.

Occasionally during a session, the client would mention an animal and I would interpret it for them. After a while I was inundated with requests for me to explain the nature of the messages from the Animal Kingdom and their personal meaning.

For example, let's look at a few of the powerful messages from the Spider:

Is there a power struggle going on in any of your relationships?

Are you dominant and overpowering in your relationships or is someone dominating you?

Are you in a no win situation?

A friend rang me up, crying because she hates spiders. I asked her what were the spiders doing? She said "There were two fat bodied spiders and one was on top of the other, rolling around my bath" **I said to her you are in a power struggle with someone, can you think of who that would be?** My friend said she'd fallen out with her best friend the night before and had a huge argument and disagreement over politics.

In my opinion **you're both very strong characters with different points of view**, it's alright for both of you to have separate and different thoughts and opinions, however you are both caught up trying to overpower one another.

You are now both at loggerheads and at battle with each other, **it's a no win situation for the both of you.** You have been best friends for over twenty years, please don't let this situation get out of control and run the risk of losing your friendship through your ego. Why don't you call her and If I was you Emily I would explain that on this occasion, can we agree to disagree? Our friendship means more than my opinion. It's ok to have our differences, we can still be good friends.

One hour later, my friend rang me, crying this time with joy that they had both made up and were back on track again, agreeing to disagree. We don't have to be a people pleaser, it's ok to have different opinions.

Fortunately, on this occasion my friend didn't see any webs as being caught up in a web could have possibly meant the end of their friendship and the fact that the spiders were big and fat signified strong egos and big problems.

Table of Contents

Ant

A hard working creature who is a member of a large infrastructure?

Ants are fascinating, the red ants, flying ants, leaf cutting ants and fire ants make up the most amazing colonies.

Ants have casts, each ant has a different role to play.

When the ant becomes ill, it gets carried back to its nest by all his colleagues.

Are you a soldier?

Do you soldier on through the toughest times?

Are you in the services?

Are you a defender?

Are you there for your friends and family, supporting and encouraging them?

Do you protect your family?

Are you loyal?

There is great strength in numbers.

Are you always prepared to work hard and do your bit?

Although at times you may feel your job isn't so significant, without you the bigger picture couldn't happen.

We all contribute to making the world go round and every single individual is needed equally to make this happen.

Be proud in whatever you do; as other people could be relying on you.

Are you hard working?

Do you know your job inside out?

Are you an achiever?

Are you strong?

Are you good at carrying things along?

Do you see things through? Ants never give up, if someone moves their nest they will all move together.

Ants don't leave people out, they all work as a team and everyone is important, they leave a trail for other ants to follow.

So are you a helper?

Are you in an organisation where you all help each other?

Are you a planet worker, benefiting everyone?

Are you complimenting someone on their work performance?

Are you doing your work for nothing, really just to help mankind?

If you see a red ant it's a warning- Is someone by you being destructive or angry?

Are protestors campaigning properly or because they like the anger, which one are you?

Are you a force to be reckoned with?

Are you part of a colony?

Are you great at taking control of things?

Are you on the attack?

Ants carry leaves to their forage.

Are you a labourer?

Are you a leaf cutter?

Are you cutting a pathway to success?

Do you own cutting edge technology?

Do you have precision timing?

Are you working on a conveyor belt?

Do you work on an assembly line?

Do you feel like a queen?

Do you get waited on hand, foot and finger?

Are you really fertile?

Are you trying to avoid work by having many children?

Is your home your nest?

Do you like travel?

Do you like to follow a trail?

Are you a tracker?

Are you a scout checking things out?

Is someone following or stalking you?

Is somebody keeping track of your movements?

Are you part of the corporate world?

Are you a great work mate?

Do you trust your work mates?

Are you in an organisation that's highly organised?

Are you a consumer?

Are you influenced by commercialism or advertising?

Is someone controlling your mind?

Are you completely loyal and true to your word?

Are you a whistle blower?

Do you like following rules?

Are you always going forward?

Are you really progressing?

Are you creating abundance?

Do you like sharing your food with friends?

Are you dominant?

Are you sociable?

Are you part of a community?

Are you detached from your emotions?

Do you have amazing intuition?

Do you have a distinctive smell?

Are you leaving a pheromone trail?

Does a certain smell trigger a response or reaction in you?

Are you extremely clean?

Are you thinking of emigrating?

Is someone tagging you?

Is your mind like a computer?

Are you great at solving problems using your logic?

Would you risk your own life for others to be safe?

Are you a great survivor?

Do you like mazes?

Do you like tunnels?

Have you got ants in your pants?

Have you got an infection?

Possible Life Paths?

Leaf Cutter, Garden Nursery Worker, Industrial Worker.

Aid Workers, Charity Workers, Miner, Engineer.

Boat Builder, Soldier, Social Organiser.

Gardener, Cook, Chef, Nurse, Waiter, Waitress, Survey Staff.

Computer Programmer, Scout, Problem Solver, Security Guard, Bouncer.

Patrol Officer, Vibrational Medicine, Paramedic, Quality Control, Life Guard, Royal Navy.

Construction Worker, Builder, Tour Guide, Tourist or Trip Information Advisor, Terrorist, Suicide Bomber.

Electrician, Plasterer or Bricklayer; all efficient workers that rely on each other.

Badger

Badgers live in burrows underground and are very family orientated in groups called Sets.

Are you living in dingy dwellings or perhaps a basement?

Are you getting enough daylight?

Are you keeping out of the light?

Do you need to lighten up?

Do you feel like a reject?

Are you out of balance?

Are you too black and white?

Can you be aggressive?

Do you change moods quickly?

Are you vicious and territorial?

Are you looking for trouble?

Do you fight over things?

Are you set in your ways?

Do you get wound up and angry over family members when normally you mind your own business?

Do family annoy you?

Are you fighting other people's battles?

Is this really your war?

Try and be tolerant of others, you can choose your friends but you can't choose your family.

Are you being too direct?

Are you fierce?

Are you like a tank or armored vehicle?

Are you extremely strong?

Are you extremely protective of your family?

Is a person badgering you or are you badgering them?

Are you annoying or antisocial?

Is someone being aggressive towards you or your family?

Do you need to sort out a situation?

Do you feel like going underground?

Are you making the wrong or dangerous connections?

Are you in an underground organisation that if came to light, you would be ashamed of your connection?

Is your organisation planning dark and secret activities?

Do you regret joining and getting involved with them?

Are you getting involved with something that's out of your depth?

Are you preying on the vulnerable and unexpected?

Are you damaging others with your extreme thoughts and behaviour?

Can you escape this life threatening cycle?

Do you have suicidal thoughts?

Have you been brainwashed?

Is deception around you?

Is someone pretending to be who they are not?

Are you in a position of trust and you've abused that power?

Remember Revelations, things will be revealed soon. The truth always comes out.

Are you getting to the bottom of the hidden or underlining problems that you haven't been able to view before?

Have you been blind folded to the truth of a situation?

Are you being led astray?

Are you being taken advantage of?

Are you seeking or seeing the truth about a situation?

Do you feel shame or guilt about something you've buried or hidden?

Are you hiding away?

Are you an offender or defender?

Are you the good guy or the bad guy?

Are you in the light or in the dark?

Do you need to find moderation?

Are you a force to be reckoned with?

Are you being destructive?

Are you a defender of your family?

Are people out to harm you or your family?

Are people wanting to kill you?

Is your work and home life in balance?

Do you like to get drunk?

Is alcohol a problem?

Do you have chest or lung problems?

Do you have balance problems?

Are you a digger?

Do you like getting to the bottom of things?

Do you like going through tunnels?

Do you need a chest X-ray?

Do you like logos or badges?

Brighten up your life with colours; give your home a nice colourful look with fresh flowers and a little splash of paint.

Do you enjoy cooking and entertaining? This is a great time to gather the family for a get together.

Possible Life Paths?

Lorry Driver, Digger Driver, Pest Control, Doctor, Nurse, Animal Protection.

Motorway Maintenance, Highways, Construction, Labourer. Trafficker, Smuggler.

Criminal Activities, Gang Warfare, Investigators, Detectives, Intelligence Officers, Cyber Crime.

Addiction and Recovery worker, Safe Guarding.

Child Protection, Family Liaison Officer, Social Worker, Refugee Advocate.

Bee

The bee has a striking black and yellow body, flying around collecting nectar from plants and flowers to make honey.

Bees don't sting unnecessarily.

Do you need to take some honey to build your immunity?

Bees make their own antibiotic.

Honey is a good replacement for sugar.

If you take a spoonful of local honey every day through the winter months, come next year your hay fever should disappear.

The bee is a symbol of abundance and fertility and the sweetness of life.

Are you making nectar?

Do you want to tell someone to buzz off?

Are you buzzing with excitement?

Do you need to take some honey?

Have you felt run down?

Have you had a cold or sore throat?

Have you had bad digestion or a stomach bug?

Maybe you've been low in energy?

Maybe you need a break to recover?

Eat, sleep and rest, look after yourself.

Are you spreading nice things, spreading honey around, good-natured?

Are you humming along to the rhythm of life?

Are you working hard?

Are you a team worker? You will soon benefit from all your hard work.

Maybe a pay rise, small windfall or a bonus, could be on its way to you shortly?

Bees go around pollinating, are you a gardener?

Are you loyal, like a body guard?

Are you working in a team, like the army?

All team workers have an important part to play.

Is your partner like a body guard to you?

Are you spending too much time at work?

Are you a hard worker?

Is your work bringing much success?

Are you always extremely busy?

Are you high maintenance?

Are you spreading the love?

Are you very fertile?

Are you trying for a baby?

Are you buzzing about something exciting?

Are you spreading abundance and love?

Are your ideas inspirational?

Does your presence make people smile and feel happy?

Bees make their own antibiotic.

Do you need a course of antibiotics?

Do you like to be a Queen Bee?

Are you a hard worker?

Are you part of a hard working team?

Have you any allergies?

Have you hives on your skin?

Do you like the colour yellow?

Have you loads of energy?

Do you love flowers?

Has someone just brought you flowers?

Do you have a sweet tooth?

Do you have to cut down on your sugar intake?

Are you addicted to fizzy drinks?

Are you dehydrated?

Are you looking at your diet and calorie intake?

Have you put on weight?

Have you lost weight?

Are you bumbling along?

Are you buzzing around?

Is all your hard work now reaping rewards?

Is your life sweet?

Would you like to look after Bees?

Would you like to make money?

Have you just come into money?

Are you about to get rich?

Allow abundance into your life!

Are you a busy Bee?

Are you a workaholic?

Do you love the sun and summer?

Are you a people pleaser?

Please yourself, you can't be all things to all
people.

Is it time to swarm into action or join forces?

Are you part of the corporate world?

Are you a consumer?

Are you influenced by commercialism or advertising?

Possible Life Paths?

Gardeners, Farmers, Agriculturist, Porter, Hotelier.

Lumberjack, Ranger, Ecologist, Forest Worker, Factory Worker.

Pilot, Soldier, Body Guard, Teacher, Shop Assistant.

Builder, Architect, Repairman, Maintenance Worker.

Butterfly

An ugly bug that turns into the most amazing insect of beauty.

Have you felt in the past that you were not so attractive? Well take a look at yourself now, you are beautiful!

The butterfly is a very positive message that you are on a journey of transformation.

Are you transforming like a butterfly?

Do you flit from one project to another?

Are you a freedom seeker?

Is someone out to deceive you?

Don't get caught up in somebody's net.

Are you flitting from one task to the next?

Have you got numerous projects on the go?

Do you start tasks and never finish them?

Does your mind never shut off?

Are you an over thinker?

Are you creative?

Is someone carrying you?

Are you extremely gentle and sensitive?

Are you a lightworker?

Are you wishing people success?

Are you spreading positivity and good fortune?

Have you been lost and now found your true self?

Have you shown your true colours?

Is someone trying to break you or pull you to pieces?

Do you like nature?

Are you transforming your life?

Are you expanding?

Are you pregnant?

Do you feel ugly?

Are you going through puberty or the menopause?

Are you experiencing life changes?

Are you a wee bit fragile?

Are you feeling delicate?

Are you beautiful?

Are you attractive?

Are people mesmerized by you?

Do you need hypnotherapy?

Are you changing?

Are you going through an ugly and painful period in your life?

Just like the caterpillar morphing into a butterfly, transformation is taking place.

Leave your past behind, let metamorphosis begin and transform your life.

Life is a forever changing cycle, nothing stays the same.

Is it time to take a new direction?

Venture out and explore new pathways.

Is it time for transformation and new beginnings?

Now is the time to create abundance.

Is your mind over active?

Are you creative?

Are you a multitasker?

Are you artistic?

Is everything boring to you?

Are you easily distracted?

Do you find it hard to make a choice?

Do you find it hard to concentrate at school?

Are you forever changing jobs?

Do you easily give up?

Are you fidgety and restless?

Are you stubborn and stuck in your negative patterns of behaviour?

Think of the **Motorway** analogy.

Left Lane=Too Slow, do you need a kick start?

Right Lane=Thrill Seeking & Danger.

Middle Lane=Balanced & Moving Forward.

Do you have numerous relationships?

Is it time to look at things from a different perspective?

Possible Life Paths?

Beautician, Ballerina, Veterinary Surgeon, Artist, Sculptor, Tattooist.

Pilot, Air Hostess, Air Force, Navy, Holiday Representative.

Personal Assistant, Nail Technician, Hair Dresser, Recruitment, Human Resources.

Designer, Multitasker, Counsellor, Psychotherapist, Addiction Counsellor.

Cat

A cat is full of wisdom and often has more than one home.

They can still be on the wild side, almost lead a double life!

Cats are very independent.

They sometimes torment and play with mice, purring and enjoying every moment.

In Egyptian times they were the seer's and protectors of secret knowledge.

Are you a hunter?

Are you a prowler?

Are you an opportunist?

Do you enjoy the company of others?

Are you rubbing people up the wrong way?

Are you full of mischief?

Are you living on the wild side?

Do you need protection?

Have you just seen a black cat? Luck maybe on its way.

Are you learning to be independent?

Are you affectionate?

Are you developing self-love?

Are you spending a lot of time on your appearance?

Are you seductive?

Is someone trying to seduce you?

Are you an offender or defender?

Are you being a bit of a Tom Cat?

Are you being too promiscuous and out of control?

Are you in a position where you cannot resist watching and enjoying the downfalls and misfortunes of others?

Are you spying on others?

Are you keeping a watchful eye on your family?

Are you a copycat?

Are you being spiteful for no reason?

Have you been sick?

Have you eaten something that's disagreed with you?

Maybe it's time for you to relax by a warm fire and chill out?

Do you need to protect yourself?

Be strong and self-reliant.

Are you taking risks with your life?

Are you leading a double life?

Are you living between two homes?

Are you in a house or flat share?

Are you in foster care?

Are you thinking of moving home?

Are you curious? Curiosity killed the cat!

Are you becoming more intuitive?

Is new knowledge coming your way?

Are you a wise soul?

Is knowledge and wisdom part of everyday life?

Are you highly intuitive?

The answers to all problems are deep within you.

Are you a seer?

Are you psychic?

Have you had a near death experience?

Are you a believer of past lives?

Do you have vivid dreams or nightmares?

Are you mysterious?

Are you superstitious?

Are you drawn to the mystery and magic of life?

Do you identify yourself as a dark or white witch?

Do you practice spells or take part in magic rituals?

Are you interested in the paranormal?

Are you trying to activate your third eye?

Do you believe in karma and the Law of Attraction?

What goes around comes around.

You reap what you sow.

Are you a healer?

Do you use herbs and natural medicines?

Are you a walking dictionary?

Are you open to new teachings?

Are you thinking of adoption?

Are you adopted?

Are you looking for someone to adore and take care of you?

Are you faithful and loyal?

Are you tempted to stray?

Are you being too territorial?

Are you in a gang?

Have you got your claws into somebody? Or has somebody got their claws into you?

Are you taking too many risks?

Are you in a risky business?

Are you running round like a flee in a fit?

Do you like being spoilt?

Is someone special spoiling you?

Do you need to treat and spoil yourself?

Do you like wearing perfume or after shave?

Possible Life Paths?

Architect, Engineer, Lawyer, Solicitor, Barrister, Attorney, Teacher, Counsellor.

Planning Officer, Auctioneer, Assembly Line Worker, Beauty Therapist,

Hairdresser, Librarian, Archaeologist, Museum Curator, Historian, Registrar, Philosopher, Perfumer.

Travel Agent, Tourist Guide, Stock Broker, Insurance, Investor Property Developer or Estate Agent?

Chicken

Is there a pecking order around you and your friends?

Are you a dare devil or are you a chicken?

Don't be influenced to do things or try things that you know are wrong.

Are you being picked on?

Is there a rotten egg around you?

Have you got egg on your face?

Have you just hatched a great idea?

Are you scratching away at something or someone?

Have you mislaid something?

Is a project you've been working on just about to hatch out?

Have you got loads of new ideas and inspirations?

Are you stuck and being prevented from achieving your goals? (Egg Bound)

Do you need a caesarean?

Are you a mother hen?

Are you broody?

This maybe a very fertile time.

Are you pregnant?

Is it time to start a family or look after someone else's children?

Are you feeling pressured to have more children?

Are you scared of a situation?

Are you running away from a situation?

Are you a freedom seeker?

Do you feel you have freedom of choice?

Are you making the right choice?

For Children Use **Traffic lights**.

● RED = STOP – Are you angry/cross? Are things not going your way?

● AMBER = THINK- Do not say or do anything.

● GREEN = GO GET HELP - Stay calm, breathe back into control. (Cause & Effect)

For adults Use the **Motorway.**

LEFT LANE = Too Slow, do you need a kick start?

RIGHT LANE = Thrill Seeking & Danger.

MIDDLE LANE = Balanced & Moving Forward.

Are you laying the road to success?

Are you controlling?

Are you being controlled?

Are you vulnerable?

Are you not being treated fairly?

Are you on the run from the police?

Are you running away from the past?

Do you want to run away from home?

Are you playing truant?

Do you need to escape from a situation?

Do you feel like you're in danger now?

Do you feel you're in a dead end job?

Are you on a low wage?

Are you scratching around to make ends meet?

Do you feel bored?

Do you feel you are battery operated?

Do you feel drained?

Do you feel like a robot?

Are you burying your head in the sand?

Have you got chicken pox or shingles?

Are you suffering a vitamin D deficiency?

Do you need sunlight & daylight?

Have you had a golden opportunity?

Possible Life Paths?

Factory Worker, Fast Food Worker, Cleaner, Assembly Line Worker.

Ticket Collector, Supermarket Assistant, Shelf Filler, Trolley Collector.

Telesales, Insurance Sales, Athlete, Child Minder.

Cow

The cow spends much of the day munching and grazing in fields watching the world go by with their beautiful, inquisitive eyes.

Have you a holy connection?

Is religion a big part of your life?

Are you allowed to make your own choices?

Are you calm and peaceful?

Do you reflect peace?

Are you on the path to enlightenment?

Are you feeling euphoric?

Have you reached enlightenment or being awakened?

Do you have compassion and empathy for humanity?

Take a truthful and honest look at your behaviour and see if it matches the Cow.

Are you trusting?

Are you a great mum?

Do you want to be a mum?

Are you fertile?

Are you thinking of breast feeding?

Are you wanting to mother everyone?

Are you an amazing parent?

Are you nurturing others?

Do you need to nurture yourself?

Are you a defender of your family?

Do you get defensive over comments made about your family?

Are you fiercely protective over your young family?

Do you feel your family members are undervalued?

Are you abundant?

Are you wise?

Do you enjoy your food?

Are you always hungry?

Do you never feel full?

Are you big and pure hearted?

Are you forgiving?

Are you a good provider?

Are you full of goodness?

Are you holistic in your approach to life?

Are you a vegan or vegetarian?

Are you passionate about animal cruelty?

Are you being treated like a piece of meat?

Are you being persecuted?

Is someone after your hide?

Are you frightened and distressed?

Do people not respect you?

Are you being disrespectful of others?

Are you treating your animal fairly?

Do you think it's ok to kill and slaughter animals?

Are you a hypocrite?

Are you in denial?

Are you ignorant to the pain and suffering of others?

Are the steaks too high?

Have you thought about donating to a RSPCA, PDSA or wild life trust?

Is it time to stop and take a look at any problems?

Stop when life is getting you down.

Meditate or pray to find the resolution.

Get out in nature and enjoy the healing of the field and the natural milk of life.

Stand strong, centre yourself, move forward with ease.

Are you a big character?

Do you have beautiful eyes?

Are you a lovely innocent soul who just loves life?

Are you content with your life?

Don't rush life, take it in and enjoy the ride.

Possible Life Paths?

Yoga Teacher, Teacher, Complimentary Medicine, Homeopath, Reflexology.

Nurse, Aid Worker, Nursey Nurse, Cobbler, Butcher, Midwife, Farmer, Agriculture.

Milkman, Grocer, Doctor, Dinner Lady, Chef, Cook, Ayurvedic Medicine, Pharmacist.

Deer

A gentle and elegant nimble, noble creature that roams wild.

The deer brings new opportunities to learn.

Are you on a new chapter of learning?

Are you on a new course?

Are you going to study something that will change your life?

Are you drawn to new adventures and horizons?

Are you going somewhere you've never been before?

Are you on the road to sustainability?

Are you back on track?

Are you thinking of emigrating abroad?

Are you thinking of relocating or working in another area?

Are you thinking of training in a new subject or starting college?

The female deer can be shy and reserved, while the male can be aggressive and confrontational.

Can you be confrontational?

Do you run at the slightest sign of trouble?

Do you get confused between aggression and being assertive?

Do you need to stand your ground?

Are you defensive?

Deer can be destructive.

Are you breaking things up that take a long time to build?

Is someone trying to destroy something you've created?

Are you being head hunted?

Does someone see you as a bit of a trophy?

Is someone hunting you down?

Do you like archery?

Are you competitive?

Are you branching out?

Are you shy?

Are you timid?

Are you in a dispute?

Have you got to show your inner strength?

Are you fighting with your sisters and brothers?

Are you protecting a female?

Are you a great athlete?

Are you great at running?

Do you like high speed?

Do you enjoy the chase?

Is life too busy for you?

Do you need to go into nature?

Do you like sunrises and sunsets?

Are you gentle and understanding?

Are you a peacemaker?

Are you an empath?

Are you a deer one?

Are you beautiful?

Are you magnificent?

Have you got good taste?

Are you living the dream?

Pay attention to your dreams.

Are you awakening?

Possible Life Paths?

Postman, Teacher, Tourist Guide, Holiday Rep, Conservationist.

Tree Surgeon, Landscape Gardener, Grounds Man, Horticulturist, Food Taster.

Dog

Dog, back to front spells GOD. A man's best friend.

A dog can survive all around the world in all different conditions.

They're extremely versatile and adaptable.

They're very good at sniffing out a situation.

Dogs are very loyal and protective of their owners.

A dog has unconditional love and affection.

Is your dog your baby?

Are you truly devoted to someone?

Is someone hopelessly devoted to you?

Are you a true and loyal friend?

Do you think you are a loyal friend?

Are you a loyal companion?

Are you good at picking up on others moods?

Are you chewing over a situation?

Are you protective over your family and friends?

Are you chasing around?

Are you snapping & biting people's heads off?

Have you just been bitten?

Have you just had a warning?

Are you feeling unwanted and uncared for?

Have you just been dumped? Or do you want to dump someone?

Are you a top dog?

Do you think you're a top dog?

Are you performing for rewards?

Are you burying things?

Do you need to exercise?

Do you attend agility or obedience classes?

Are you obedient?

Are you a conformist?

Are you stepping out of line?

Do you enjoy watching tricks?

Are you tricking others?

Do you need to make some life style changes?

Are you grinding your teeth?

Are you spot on with your intuition?

Do you know who you can trust?

Have you got a sixth sense, can you sniff a situation out?

Do you trust your instincts?

Do you strongly judge others?

Are you highly intelligent?

Do you have a strong sense of smell?

Are you a people pleaser?

Are you submissive?

Are you giving in too easily?

Do you want to go your separate way?

Are you pining?

Do you spend time crying or howling?

Are you being controlled?

Are you being trained to act violently?

Are you irritating to someone?

Are you loud and annoying your neighbours?

Have you got an unhealthy attachment?

Are you co-dependent?

Are you inseparable?

Do you like being on your own?

Are you lonely?

Are you feeling lost?

Do you want your own space?

Are you at the beck and call of others?

Do you jump at the commands of others? If so how high?

Do you want to run away?

Are you on the run?

Who are you running to or what are you running from?

Are you trying to escape?

Are you being groomed?

Do you have a strong sexual urge for a certain person?

Are you a dirty dog?

Are you sniffing around?

Possible Life Paths?

Manager, Chief Exec, Military Officer, Police Chief, Police Officer, Prison Officer, Soldier.

Bomb Disposal, Airport Security, Dog Handler. Body and Security Guards, Surgeons, Doctors.

Nurses, Therapists, Teacher, Lecturer, Professor, Lawyer.

Solicitor, Barrister, Attorney, Judge, Chef, Waitress, Butler, Servant.

Cooks, General Service Professions, Personal Trainers, Instructors, Sports Athletes.

Donkey

Donkeys work extremely hard and can be stubborn.

Are you doing all the donkey work?

Are people burdening your work load?

Are you being overloaded?

Are you feeling like a pack horse donkey?

Are people expecting too much work from you?

Are you taking too much work on?

Are you exhausted from work?

Are you a people pleaser? Learn to say **NO**.

Has your work brought you to a stop?

Has your energy gone and your health been affected?

Are you burnt out?

Do you have panic or anxiety attacks?

Do you have a low immune system?

Do you feel under pressure from others?

Do others use and abuse you?

Do people bully or make fun of you?

Are you surrounded by other's selfishness?

Do others expect way too much of your time and energy?

Are people on your back?

Are you feeling burdened?

Do you have back or shoulder problems?

Do you carry the world on your shoulders?

Have you been the high flyer who now just wants the simplicity of life?

Are you seeking freedom?

Are you wanting to go trekking or on a journey?

Do you need to relax and take time out?

Are you needing a rest or wanting a holiday?

Do you need to take walks in nature?

Do you like the seaside?

Do you feel like the joker or are you the joke?

Are you being stubborn or stuck in your ways?

Are you being too rigid?

Are you a fool or is somebody treating you like one?

Are you feeling emotional?

Do you feel like crying?

Have you really good hearing?

Are you good at multitasking?

Do you suffer with ear problems?

Do you listen?

Is your past catching up with you?

Are you running away from your past?

Have you turned your back on the past?

Are people always on your case?

Do friends take advantage of you?

Is the responsibility of family or friends breaking you?

Have people just got used to you doing everything for them?

Are you being treated fairly and with respect?

Have you been thinking about a pension?

Have you thought about your retirement and where you would like to travel?

Do you want to give money to a donkey sanctuary or good cause?

Possible Career Paths?

Shop Assistant, Cleaner, Waitress, Kitchen Hand.

Car Valet, Nursery Nurse, Kids Entertainer, Fast Food Worker.
Farm Hand, Fruit Picker, Factory Worker, Personal Assistant.

Hotel Staff, Coach Driver, Airport Staff, Baggage Handlers.

Dove/Pigeon

The sign of this pure white bird is heaven coming down to earth.

The Dove is a sign of unconditional love, peace and hope.

Are you peaceful or making peace?

Are you gentle?

Are you highly sensitive?

Are you pure and trustworthy?

Do you speak your truth?

Are you working with integrity and for the good of others?

Are you seeking tranquility and serenity?

Are you a freedom seeker?

Are you restless?

Is life too noisy?

Are you at war?

Have you been affected by war?

Have you gone to war?

Is this really your fight?

Are you intolerant to other's religious beliefs or views?

Are your views racist?

Are you ignorant or prejudice to other cultures?

Are you accepting of different faiths?

Are you angry with GOD?

Are you angry in your heart?

Do you need to make peace with others?

Are you at peace with yourself?

Do you need to reconnect to humanity?

Do you need to practice selflessness?

It's time to treat others as yourself.

Do you need to forgive others?

Have you just been forgiven?

Do you need to offer the olive branch of forgiveness?

Do you need to forgive yourself?

Are you seeking revenge?

Be mindful of the law of cause and effect, what goes around comes around.

Are you a victim?

Have you been damaged or traumatized by life?

Do you need rescuing?

Are you in a safe house?

Are you in temporary accommodation?

Are you homeless or a refugee?

Are you fleeing from a dangerous situation?

Are you feeling drained and exhausted?

Are you feeling delicate or fragile?

Is someone ruffling up your feathers?

Are your thoughts pure?

Are you being tempted by the dark?

Is someone trying to blacken your reputation?

Are you seeking the light?

Have you been suffering in silence?

Are you going through life's challenges or obstacles?

Are you going through life's changes?

Has someone close to you just died?

Are you finding it hard to deal with the loss of a loved one?

Have you lost a child?

Are you feeling stressed?

Do you feel anxious and nervous?

Have you been flooded?

Are your emotions overwhelming you?

Do you find it hard to express your emotions?

Does the thought of dealing with your emotions frighten you?

Are you suffering from PSTD?

Do you have negative or dark thoughts?

Do you have suicidal thoughts?

Are you self-harming?

Are addictions masking your pain?

Do you suffer with OCD, panic or anxiety attacks?

Have you ever thought of counselling or CBT (Cognitive Behavioral Therapy)?

Or the practice of meditation and mindfulness?

Do you need to work on self-acceptance or forgiveness?

Do you suffer from insomnia?

Are you sensitive to what you here?

Have you forgotten to relax?

Do you need family or relationship therapy?

Do you need a mediator?

Do you hate criticism?

Are people jealous of you?

Are you waiting for results?

Do others feel safe and calm around you?

Are you feeling euphoric?

Have you reached enlightenment or been awakened?

Do you have compassion and empathy for humanity?

Take a truthful and honest look at your behaviour and see if it matches the Dove.

Are you your authentic self?

Do you have a strong connection to God, Jesus or Mother Mary?

It is time for us all to join together as one!

Possible Life Paths?

Counsellor, Psychologist, Psychiatrist, Life Coach, Carer, Social/Aid Worker, Teacher.

Negotiator, Mediator, Judge, Arbitrator, Librarian, Olive Grower.

Peace/Human Rights Campaigners, Hospice Worker, Vet, Nun, Monk.

Any profession that requires the calmness, integrity and empathy of a Dove.

Duck

A cute little bird with gorgeous coloured feathers.

The duck loves to swim in ponds and marsh areas, quacking away.

Ducks look very calm on the surface of the water but their legs are paddling like mad under water.

Do you suffer from anxiety?

Do you look calm but deep inside of you it's another story?

Do you have hidden emotions?

Are you feeling emotional?

Can you not face your emotions?

Do you want to hide your emotions from others?

Do you enjoy the outdoors?

Do you like water sports?

Have you thought about learning to swim?

Do you need healing?

Do you like the company of your family and spending time out with them?

Are you noisy?

Is your family noisy?

Are you gentle?

Does life seem a bit harsh?

Are you trying to stay out of trouble?

Are you a sitting duck?

Are you a target?

Are you vulnerable?

Do you need to call for help? We all need help sometimes.

Are you finding your feet?

Do you have problems with your feet?

Do you not like facing problems?

Do you have secrets?

Are you being honest?

Honesty is the best policy.

Do you have freedom to go where you want?

Do you have freedom of choice?

Are you using avoidance?

Are you standing up for yourself?

Are you being a coward?

Tell someone if you are not happy or being bullied.

Have you a large family to look after?

Does the responsibility overwhelm you?

Do you feel misunderstood?

Do you dislike busy places?

Are you seeking peace?

Are you expecting trouble?

Do you feel threatened by others?

Do you need to go with the flow?

Are you going with the flow of life or are you going against it?

Maybe change direction, don't always follow other people, be independent.

Are you ducking and diving?

Is someone ducking and diving from you? Why is that?

Do you feel the cold?

Would you like to go to a warmer climate in the winter months?

Are people after you, making a meal out of you, do they want to get you?

Have you got your head just above the water?

Are you getting into trouble by opening your mouth?

Have you talked out of turn?

Are you frozen with fear?

Has something given you a scare?

Are you short of money?

Are you finding times difficult?

Don't take risks with your life or money.

Are you diving in to new experiences or opportunities?

Are you pregnant?

Are you a great parent?

Do you need swimming lessons, water sports, diving lessons?

Try canoeing lessons and become a water baby!

Maybe you need to go to a river for peacefulness.

Learn to relax.

Possible Life Paths?

Diving Instructor, Swimming Instructor, Life Guard, Water Sports Instructor.

Gym Instructor, Chef, Receptionist, Office Worker, Sailor, Ship Crew.

Wheeler Dealer, Con Man.

Earth Worm

The earth worm spends all day and night churning the soil and continuously going round and round.

The earth worm is consistently oxygenating and aerating the earth.

Are you going round and round?

Are you repeating the same cycle or patterns in life?

Are you making the same mistakes and getting the same experiences?

Are you stuck in a cycle of negativity?

Are you repeatedly churning up the same stuff?

Are you going over the same ground?

Are you constantly telling the same story?

Don't dwell in the past, just leave it behind.

Are you scared to try new things?

Do you identify yourself as a victim?

Do you feel life is against you?

Are you always making excuses for your misery?

Are you waiting for someone else to change your life?

Do you feel you are going around in the dark?

Move out of the darkness & towards the light.

Do you feel you're getting nowhere in life?

Have you lost your direction in life?

Do you feel lack of recognition?

Are you unaware of who you truly are?

Do you always see the glass as half empty?

Are you hiding away from reality?

Stop hiding away, let yourself be heard!

Are you being weedy or needy?

Do you feel you're being used as bait?

Have you just opened up a can of worms?

Is someone making you squirm & cringe?

Is your negative thinking affecting your physical health?

Watch your thoughts!! Your mind is very powerful!

Try and be in the here and now, focus on the **NOW**.

Are you unforgiving? This can create bitterness.

Un-forgiveness is very toxic and acidic & may cause great harm to your health.

Are you aware of how your behaviour affects others?

Do you need anger management?

Take responsibility of your health.

Are you a shallow breather? Practice deep breathing.

Do you need oxygen?
Focus on the breath and breathing exercises.

What haven't you learnt?

Are you repeating the same lessons in life?

Learn by your past mistakes. If you keep doing the same things, you'll continually get the same results.

Remember **KEY:**

Knowledge Empowers You

Are you fed up doing the same career, maybe time for a change?

Step out of your comfort zone, try something new.

Are you slippery or slimy?

Are you about to slip up?

Does someone give you the shivers?

Have you recently just split up?

Do you feel cut up about a situation?

Do you need to cut ties from an unhealthy situation?

Are you lonely and in despair?

Are you grieving?

Do you need bereavement counselling?

Do you need life coaching or Cognitive Behaviour Therapy?

Are you feeling fidgety and wriggly?

Are you restless or bored?

Do you have unknown fears or phobias?

Do you need your eyes tested?

Possible Life Paths?

Factory, Assembly Worker, Miner, Singer, Grounds man, Life Coach, Registrar, Court Usher.

Car Dealer, Cowboy Builder, Market Seller, Wheeler Dealer, Con Man, Trading Standards Officer, Fraud Investigation.

Any repetitive and monotonous job.

Fox

The fox is a magical, intelligent creature, with sharp senses and intellect.

Foxes are very adaptable to town/country.

Are you a good provider?

Are you a good planner?

Are you swift & quick to make decisions?

Are you an opportunist?

Is your behaviour dodgy or shifty?

Are you a bounder or a scoundrel?

Are you a thief?

Do you need to invest in a burglar alarm or surveillance and security system?

Are you self-centered?

Do you hide your true feelings or emotions?

Do you feel exhausted by others around you?

Are people chasing you?

Are you chasing around?

Are you a scavenger?

Are you calculating and manipulative?

Is your behaviour treacherous or vicious?

Are you striking out or can you be cruel?

Are you ruthless, planning to take someone out?

Are you leaving a horrific trail of destruction?

Is your behaviour trying to shock people?

Are you crossing or pushing boundaries?

Are you watching and ready to instantly respond?

Are you in the right place at the right time?

Are you a patient planner?

Are you playing the waiting game?

Are you very versatile and adaptable?

Are you out in all weathers?

Do you have a quick, sharp mind?

Are you cunning?

Can you out smart others?

Are you diverting people?

Do you have OCD?

Are rituals part of your everyday life?

Are you opening up to psychic awareness?

Are you becoming more intuitive?

Are you being promiscuous? Take precautions & look after yourself.

Is sex always on your mind?

Have you a sex addiction?

Are you a lady of the night?

Are you having an affair?

Are you thinking about having an affair?

Are you feeling rough?

Are you reckless, wild or out of control?

Are you untamable?

Do you feel battered by life?

Do you feel exhausted?

Have you got bad habits that are affecting your health? Check your diet.

Are people ganging up on you?

Are you a victim?

Do you feel vulnerable?

Do you feel trapped?

Nowhere to hide?

Are you running out of places to escape or hide?

Do you feel exposed?

Are you on the run?

Are you tired of running?

Are you hungry or out in the cold?

What are you running from?

Are you a natural born survivor?

Is the "survival of the fittest" testing you?

Are you prepared to beg, steal or borrow?

Are you addicted to gaming?

Are you addicted to gambling on line?

What are you trying to prove?

Are you being judged?

Are you hated?

Do you have secret knowledge?

Learn to follow your intuition and gut feelings.

The sight of a Fox can mean mystery, magic and ancient knowledge.

Are you thinking of becoming a parent?
You're going to be natural and great at it.

Are you the hirer and firer?

Are you rushing around at work?

Does your presence make people tremble?

Do people fear you?

Are you taking advantage of others?

Are you ignorant to the pain and suffering of others?

Are you making a name for yourself?

Have you got people despising you for no reason?

Are you hiding something?

Will you stop at nothing to get your own way?

Are you family orientated?

Is your weakness your family?

Is your family making too much noise?

Are you annoying your neighbours?

Are you being a bad neighbour?

Do you have anti-social behaviour?

Do you like driving at high speed?

Are you afraid of commitment?

Possible Life Paths:

Drug dealers, Stock brokers, Insurance salespeople, Wheeler and Dealer.

Conman, Bookies, Ruthless Boss, Bailiff, Debt Collector, Loan Sharks.

Traffic Warden, Tax Inspector, Body Guards, Terrorist, Media Representative.

Gang Member, Specially Trained Soldier, Under cover Journalist.

Whistleblower. Troller, Planning Enforcement Officer, Security Guard,

Farmer, Politician, Private Investigator, Law Enforcement.

Paparazzi, Cowboy Worker, Hacker, Office Mole, Charlatan.

Fly

A fly is always hovering around. A fly is irritating and annoying to others, but a message in disguise.

Flies get our attention by humming around.

Get the message, and it will leave you alone!

Are you spreading negative energy?

Have you been affected by someone's negative energy?

Are you flitting from one thing to another?

Are you irritated by someone or a situation?

Are you irritating to others?

Do you attract negative situations?

Are you attracting the same negative experience?

How can you get out of this situation?

Are you being clean and tidy?

Are you spreading disease?

Are you being contaminated by others or are you contaminating others?

Are you being hygienic?

Are you attracting flies within your living environment?

Is your kitchen a mess?

Do you need to spring clean?

Do you need your eyes tested?

Are you seeing or not seeing the true picture?

Is something nasty going on around you?

Have you got a dirty habit?

Have you caught something from someone else?

Are you in a messy situation?

Have you caused this mess?

Are you fed up of clearing up after other people?

Are you always in the shit?

Is someone out to swat you?

Is somebody causing or giving you shit?

Are you gossiping behind others backs or is somebody gossiping about you?

Are you a victim of domestic abuse or violence?

Are you being black mailed?

Has somebody got some information about you that you wouldn't want made public?

Are you dishing the dirt?

Have you put a photograph or message on line that you'd later regret?

Watch your comments on social media!

Is someone spreading rumours about you?

Is someone out to cause trouble and destroy your reputation?

Is somebody telling lies about your character or trying to get you a bad reputation?

Is someone trying to blacken your name?

Where there's muck there's money.

Do you feel trapped?

Have you set a trap to catch somebody out?

Is somebody out to trap you?

Do you feel creeped out by someone?

Is somebody creeping and crawling around you?

Explore any irritations in your relationships.

Something or somebody needs your full attention now.

Pay attention to the small print.

Possible Life Paths?

Optician, Dermatologist, Plastic Surgeon, Pest Controller.

Cleaner, Refuse Collector, Aid Worker, House Clearer, Security, Wheeler Dealer.

Paparazzi, Journalist, Doctor, Nurse,

Any profession that handles life's irritations.

Frog

A frog likes to spend its time near ponds and water.

They also hide under pebbles and rocks.

The frog likes to hop and jump about.

Are you having any throat problems?

Have you any respiratory problems?

Maybe it's time to learn to breathe properly?

Try meditation, yoga, pilates or join the choir?

Are you croaking?

Do you need time out by the sea?

If this is not possible, treat yourself to a nice spa break.

Try sea salt and seaweed spa treatments.

Is it time to take singing or swimming lessons?

Are you pregnant?

Are you experiencing fertility problems?

Be aware of how fertile you are.

Is communication a problem for you?

Does the thought of presenting in front of an audience frighten you?

Do you need coaching for public speaking?

Do you need to speak your truth?

The truth will set you free!

Are you hopping forward in leaps and bounds?

Are you hiding your talents under a stone?

Believe in yourself & your abilities!

Are you hopping from one thing to another?

Are you hopping with anger?

Is your life stagnant? Hop forward!

Break free from unwanted clutter.

Are you feeling bogged down?

Have you had some emotional setbacks?

Take a leap forward to new beginnings.

Is it time to take a leap of faith?

Is it your dream to visit the rainforest?

Do you need healing?

Are you being too competitive?

Do you avoid competition?

Take a leap forward & leave your competitors behind!

Are you futuristic and adaptable?

Are you resilient and persevering?

Do you keep changing jobs?

Do you work for yourself or considering self-employment?

Are you keeping an eye on your investments & savings?

Do you handle your finances wisely?

Are you hopping from one bed to another?

Do you need to take precautions?

Are you scared of commitment?

Are you always on the move?

Are you restless?

Are you being unfaithful?

Are you waiting for a prince or a princess?

Do you like kissing?

Do you suffer from any skin problems?

Do you need protection from the sun?

Are you dehydrated?

Are you drinking enough water?

Possible Life Paths:

Agency/temp worker or Contractor, Sales Rep
Flight Attendant, Entertainer, Presenter.

Comedian, Singer & Backing Singer, Travel Rep,
Yoga/Fitness Instructor.

Life/Voice Coach, Master of Ceremonies, TV Host, Town Crier, Voice Over Artist.

Goat

Goats can butt you, be bad tempered and hot headed.

They eat anything in sight, including washing off a clothes line!

Are you hungry all the time?

Are you toxic?

Is your diet affecting your behaviour?

Are you thinking of becoming a vegan or a vegetarian?

Are you headstrong and climbing up the ladder of life?

Have you just got a promotion? Be careful not to tread on people on your way up as those people will still be there when you come back down!

Keep that wild enthusiasm up but don't be pushy!

Are you judging others and looking down your nose at them?

Is your behaviour unpredictable and unstable?

Are you determined to get your own way?

Have you lost your direction?

Are you not listening or not taking good advice from others?

Are you pretending to be someone you're not?

Are you ignoring a problem, hoping it would disappear and go away?

Are you in denial?

Time to take responsibility and action now.

Do you feel you're a misunderstood teenager?

Are you independent and thinking outside the box?

Is your life chaotic and disruptive?

Do you get temper tantrums when others don't see your way?

Do you have mood swings?

Are you trying to distract others or is someone distracting you?

Is your life chaotic?

Are you a creator of chaos?

Are you a saboteur?

Are you being controlled or are you a control freak?

Has somebody got a hold over you?

Is your behaviour frightening to others?

Are you a self-harmer?

Does someone want to cut your throat?

Does someone want to cut you up?

Are you going through puberty or the menopause?

Are you thinking of having fertility treatment?

Are you questioning your sexuality?

Are you a cross gender?

Do you feel you are in the wrong body?

Have you thought of changing your appearance?

Do you need to either embrace your femininity or masculinity?

Are you a cross dresser?

Is someone telling you what to wear?

Are you sleeping with the enemy?

Are you somebody's trophy?

Have you or someone around you got OCD?

Are you trying to use aggression to get your own way?

Are you using humour and laughter to cover up your present pain.

Are you overwhelmed, trying to establish your identity?

Have you got a personality disorder?

Are you belittling people? Do you think you're better than everyone else?

Are you being destructive?

Are you leaving a trail of devastation?

Take a look at yourself and how your behaviour affect's others.

Can you take a joke? Or are you the joke? Lighten up.

Have you ever eaten goat's cheese or milk?

Does your body hair worry you?

Do you need to shave?

Have you started shaving?

Possible Life Paths?

Acting, Stand Up Comedian, Performing Artist, Amateur Dramatics.

Circus Entertainer, Holiday Rep, DJ, Nursery Nurse, Child Minder, Baby Sitter.

Nanny, Magician, Children's Entertainer.

Counselling, Psychologist, Psychotherapist.

Hamster

Hamsters go round and round repeating the same cycle of life.

Are you repeating that same negative cycle and pattern of behaviour?

Are you going round and round on the wheel of life?

Are you still stuck and grinding along on the wheel?

Are you making the same mistakes and getting the same experiences?

Are you having the same painful lessons?

Have you not learnt by now?

Are you on the wheel of fortune?

Are you being cheeky?

Are you bored?

Do you feel boring to other people?

Are you timid and shy?

Do you spend lots of time on your own?

Do you feel lonely and cut off from others?

Do you enjoy your own company?

Do you go over and over the same things in your mind?

Are you squabbling and fighting in your relationships?

Do you look cute but have a vicious side?

Have you got your teeth in to someone?

Are you trying to bite someone's head off?

Are you trying to kill someone?

Are you in danger?

Do you suffer from insomnia?

Do you have a broken sleep pattern?

Are you a shift worker?

Are you staying up late working?

Do you take risks at night?

Are your night time activities putting you at risk?

Are you jealous or envious of other people?

Do you hoard things?

Are you being over greedy?

Are you a binger?

Do you have odd habits, eating in the middle of the night?

Are you nocturnal in your habits?

Are you in a dead end job?

Is it time to learn new skills?

Do you have problems with your teeth?

Do you need a visit to the dentist?

Do you need your blood pressure tested?

Possible Life Paths?

Night Worker, Porter, Fast Food, Pizza Delivery, Waiter, Waitress.

Factory Worker, Cinema Attendant, Arcade and Casino Worker.

Launderette Assistant, Drug Dealer, Bouncer, Doorman.

Telesales, Customer Service Representative.

Any monotonous job.

Hawk/Eagle

This magnificent and powerful bird rules the sky as it glides gracefully through the clouds, sweeping down on its prey.

The bird has excellent vision and precision, in order to spot all opportunities with speed and accuracy.

He is a high flyer with amazing patience and spiritual awareness.

Are you aiming high?

Are your expectations or goals too high and unrealistic?

Is it time to view things from a different perspective? Take another look.

Have you felt the presence of a relative who's passed over?

Have you had a vision?

Do you feel you're being guided from up above?

Have you been thinking of embarking on a vision quest?

Are you drawn to prayer or meditation?

Have you been thinking of studying philosophies or ancient teachings i.e. Buddhism, Hinduism and Shamanism?

Are you realising your true life purpose?

Are you looking down on others?

Are you a truth seeker?

Are you getting in touch with your higher self?

Are you seeking the meaning of life?

Are you a free spirit?

Is your spirit soaring?

Have you just found something?

Have you just uncovered something?

Have you just found a long lost item?

Have you got your sight set on someone or something?

Set your goals and go for it!

Are you a quick decision maker?

Timing is crucial!

Can you see the bigger picture?

Are you seeing the true picture or are you looking through rose colour spectacles?

Are you a problem solver or troubleshooter?

Have you got problems and you see no way out?

Take a different perspective, and see through the illusions.

Look for positive solutions and outcomes, follow your intuition.

Do you live beyond your budget? Keep a watchful eye on your expenses.

Do you have thoughts of grandeur?

Are you living beyond your means?

Do you think you're a cut above other people?

Do you need a DNA test?

Are you looking into your family history or tree?

Are you a hunter?

Are you a sniper?

Are you getting your claws into something, or is something getting its claws into you?

Are you using your great strength and power to intimidate others?

Are others intimidating you?

Are you being bossy?

The hawk is in perfect harmony and balance.

Are you feeling out of balance?

Are you lacking in iron?

Are you strong and self-reliant?

Are you focused and determined?

Are you a trend setter?

Do you feel trapped?

Are you a freedom seeker?

Are you seeking the truth?

Do you need house or car insurance?

Are you about to sign a contract or important document? Beware of the small print, read it thoroughly.

Keep a watchful eye on any investments.

Beware of the pay day loans!

Are you a shopaholic?

Are you focusing too much on materialism?

Birds of Prey have amazing vision. Their targeting is spot on.

Are you due an eye check?

Look after and protect your eyes.

Could you be keeping a more watchful eye on your family?

Do you need to keep an eye on someone? i.e. Neighbour, Friends.

Have you got your eye on someone?

Have you got a secret crush?

Do you feel powerless? Step into your power.

Are people drawn to your powerful presence?

Are you turned on by people in power?

Is there a power struggle going on in your life?

Do you get a lot of attention and admiration from others?

Are you photo sensitive to certain lighting?

Possible Life Paths?

Recruitment, Head Hunter, Talent Spotter. Police, Criminal Investigator, Forensic Scientist.

Project Worker, Boss, Chief Executive, Managing Director.

Proof Reader, Examiner, Inspector, Analyst, Problem Solver, Troubleshooter.

Courier, Postman, Architect, Time & Motion Officer.

Registrar, Optician, Surgeon, Health & Safety Officer, Paramedic, First Aider.

Negotiator, Liquidator, Auditor, Accountant, Archaeologist, Antiques Dealer.

Car Dealer, Precision Engineer, Solicitor, Judge & Barrister.

Hedgehog

A spiky little creature that goes into a ball when disturbed and comes out at night.

Are you making somebody else prickly?

Do you go straight into defence mode when challenged?

Is your quickest form of defence to attack!

Is someone annoying you?

Are you about to hurt someone or harm yourself?

Are you inflicting pain on others or is someone inflicting pain on you?

Are you being crushed by other people?

Are you hiding away?

Are you in denial?

Is it time to face up to things and work things through?

Are you taking driving lessons?

Have you just passed your test?

What is your road sense like?

Are you safe on the road?

Are you a boy racer?

Is your driving fast and furious?

People tell jokes about hedgehogs but I'd like to think they're teaching us to drive slower.

Are you crossing the road without looking for vehicles?

Are you jay walking?

Cross the road in the safest place, stop, look and listen at all times.

Does your vehicle need maintenance?

Have you had a problem recently with fleas?

Who's got under your skin?

Who's irritating you? You're attracting things to get under your skin.

Are you moody?

Are people wary of your moods?

Are you trying to look happy and really want to curl up in a ball?

Is it time to deal with those hidden emotions?

Is it time to face up to things?

Do you have any mental health problems?

Do you feel depressed?

Are you a day dreamer?

Are you going around in a world of your own?

Can you not sense danger?

Do you not want to be seen in the day?

Why are you coming out in the night and not in the day?

Maybe you need more sleep and daylight?

Do you spend hours sleeping?

Are you always half asleep?

Are you suffering from insomnia or sleep deprivation?

Do you just love staying in bed?

Are you frightened to show people the real you?

Are you cute?

Do you need rescuing?

Possible Life Paths?

Doctor, Receptionist, Customer Services Representative, Pest Controller.

Furniture Salesman, Arbitrator, Family Liaison.

Paramedic, Nurse, Road Traffic Safety Officer, Animal Rescue.

Horse

Man depended on their horse for means of transportation before cars were invented.

People's status was judged by the quality of the horse they owned, as people are judged by the cars they drive today.

The farming industry were totally reliant on their horses.

Are you about to change or buy a new car?

Do you enjoy racing?

Are you in a hurry? Be careful, if you go too fast you may fall down.

Are you on the wild side?

Do you see yourself as a bit of a stallion?

Do you have a strong sex drive and feel you're a bit of a stud?

Are you feeling frisky?

Are you strong and highly intelligent?

Are you balanced, intuitive and a good judge of character?

Do you see yourself as hardworking and willing?

Can you be stubborn?

Have you got loads of stamina and inner strength?

Can you jump successfully over the hurdles of life?

Are you agile and flexible?

Are you athletic?

The horse moves forward with grace and elegance.

A willing horse carries the heaviest load.
Learn to say NO sometimes.

Do you always clean up other people's mess?

Are you ready to say enough is enough, you're expecting way too much of me?

Have you come to a halt in your life?

Are you good at understanding and working with others with disabilities, trauma, PTSD?

Do you like gambling?

Do you like a bet?

Do you like casinos?

Are the odds for or against you?

Do you bet against all odds?

Can you afford to lose?

Are you running up debts?

Do you always borrow off others or are you always lending people money?

Are you wary of others?

Are you nagging someone?

Do you keep repeating yourself?

Are you a trainer?

Do you like training?

Is someone trying to teach you new skills?

Are you a good or difficult student?

Are you a jockey?

Do you love horses?

Are you great at running?

Do you like winning a race?

Are you quick off the mark?

Do you like the chase?

Are you moving forward?

Are you handsome or a poser?

Do you enjoy wearing nice clothes?

Do you like looking smart?

Do you enjoy your hair being styled?

Are you on your best behaviour?

Are all eyes on you?

Are you being judged?

Are you judging others?

Are you checking somebody out?

Do you have an outer beauty and an inner strength?

Are you graceful?

Are you magnificent?

Is the horse world your life/status?

Are you the star of the show?

Are you high and mighty?

Do you like entering competitions?

Are you competitive?

Do you always have to be first?

Have you just won a competition?

Are you fearless at competing?

Are you heading for a fall?

Are you confident?

Have you worked to achieve your lifestyle?

Are you a gold digger?

Have you got your eye on a wealthy suitor?

Are you somebody else's trophy?

Are you someone else's bit on the side?

Are you in a love triangle?

Do you feel frisky?

Are you knackered?

Are you willing?

Are you controlled?

Is someone hitting you?

Are you a control freak?

Is someone breaking your spirit?

Is someone breaking you in or down?

Is someone showing you who's boss?

Do you have large teeth?

Are you sensitive to noise?

Have you been spoofed lately?

Have you had a fall recently?

Are you a lovely loyal friend?

Do you like making friends?

Do others put all their faith in you?

Do you have a special bond, understanding and friendship with your partner/horse?

Do you have high hopes and high expectations of yourself or of others?

Is someone asking you to jump and you say "How High?"

Do others want you to perform?

Do you love exercise?

Are you head strong?

Do you want your own way?

Have you lost your direction, just plodding along?

Are you a plodder?

Have you got enough stamina?

Have you got a strong inner core and patience of a saint?

Are you taking the lead?

Are you the first point of contact?

Are you a freedom seeker?

Do you crave freedom?

Do you love the countryside?

Do you want to gallop into the sunset?

Are you going on a journey?

Is it time to change direction?

Horses for courses. Are you on the right course in your life?

Is it time to take a leap of faith?

Are you highly intuitive?

Are you ahead of your time?

Is it time to believe in yourself?

The time to trust and believe in yourself is now!

Are life's obstacles blocking your progress?

Raise the bar, expect more good things from life?

Are you under pressure?

Are you chewing over things?

Do you need to rest?

Do you need to protect your head?

Have you just kicked off?

Do you want to kick out?

Have you just kicked someone into touch?

Do you need new shoes?

Have you got amazing hair?

Possible Life Paths?

Cobbler, Dentist, Dress Maker, Jockey, Farrier, Events Coordinator.

Competition Planner, Boss, Trainer, Personal Trainer, Physiotherapist.

Sports Massage Therapist, Book Maker, Ticket Sales, Car Sales.

Hairdresser, Beautician, Gym Instructor, Neurosurgeon.

Ladybird

The lady bird is associated with luck! Count the spots on the lady birds back; this is the number of wishes you could ask for.

If you have asked a question, the spots can represent days, months or years, the time to wait for your question to be answered!

A Ladybird signifies harmony and balance between the material and spiritual.

Wishes, dreams and aspirations take time to come together, teaching us patience.

Our belief system and patterns of behaviour are all linked or connected to our childhood experiences and expectations.

The ladybird encourages you to live your dreams and grow.

The ladybird eats pests, getting rid of irritations in life.

Are you feeling lucky?

Are you making the most of the opportunities available to you?

Are you always in the right place at the right time?

Are you thinking of flying?

Are you taking off?

Are you spreading your wings?

Are you thinking of moving?

Have you got hidden anger or frustrations?

Do you see red?

Seeing red could be warning you to rectify your anger and behaviour.

If you want to step back into your power or be noticed, wear the colour red.

Have you got any family issues?

Do you need to reconnect with your family members?

Is family everything to you?

Have you wished for something lately?

Have you made a wish list?

Are you taking care of yourself sexually?

Are you being promiscuous?

Are you a lady of the night?

Are you very sexual?

Are you full of passion?

Are you going around focusing on your own desires and wishes?

Be determined like the Ladybird. Believe in yourself.

One Acorn can turn into a huge Oak Tree, so Ladybird's remind us to stay positive over our aspirations, goals and dreams.

This is a positive sign as lady luck is shining on you in all areas of your life. So be careful what you wish for!

Ladybird is always about luck, right place right time, possibly money coming to you, the right opportunities presenting themselves.

If you're thinking of starting a new business or changing careers, now's the time.

The more ladybirds you spot the more luck that's coming your way!

Are you thinking of starting a family? Count your blessings, you could have great parenting skills.

Is it time to get some fertility advice?

Do you need to research your family tree?

Are you or somebody around you expecting a baby?

Are you creating abundance?

Do you need to reconnect to nature?

Do you need to brighten up your living environment?

Do you suffer with warts or fungal infections? Black spots can be negativity.

Is there a part of your body that is inflamed or infected?

Possible Life Paths?

Entrepreneur, Celebrity, Music, Acting, Dancing, Performing. Beautician, Model, Colour Therapist.

Advertising, Producer, Landscape Gardner, Family Planning Advisor, Painter & Decorator.

Travel Representative, Interior Designer, Life Coach, Public Speaking, TV Presenter.

Any job in the spot light.

Lion

The lion is a regal and majestic looking animal with a wonderful, strong and powerful presence.

The king of the cats!

The lion demonstrates leadership, authority and justice.

The lioness is a great mother and together the lion and lioness truly are the king and queen of the jungle.

The lioness depicts courage and grace.

Do you need courage or are you courageous?

Are you showing great strength of character?

Are you the king or queen of the jungle?

Are you being over dominant?

Are you becoming a bully?

Are you a big force to be reckoned with?

Do you put others in their place?

Are you aggressive?

Are you intimidating to others?

Do you roar and upset people around you?

Are you being snappy or aggressive?

Are you fearless?

Do you need to look after your heart?

Anger and aggression could possibly cause heart problems.

Are you posing or showing off your physique?

Do you have family troubles or issues?

Do you let your partner do all the work?

Do you take on too much work of your own?

Are you so proud you can't ask for help?

Have you been fighting?

Are you sick and tired of fighting other people's battles?

Have you exhausted your resources?

If you are in a legal dispute, justice will be done.

Have you got a job of high and mighty status?

Are you good at delegating and taking control of a situation?

Are you having the lion's share of the business?

Are you being under valued in business?

Do people value your true worth?

Has someone in business had you over?

Are you summoning up someone?

Are you being overbearing or overpowering to others?

Are you cuddly and sweet?

Do people love and adore you?

Do you make others feel protected and secure?

Are you a strong leader?

Are you a strong character?

Do you have strong views?

Do you automatically take charge?

Are you a natural born leader?

Do you roar when you're angry?

Are you handling your emotions?

Do you intimidate others?

Are you a Lionheart?

Are you big hearted?

Have you lost your strength and heart?

Is your character being put to the test?

Are you being a fair parent?

Do you demonstrate good parenting skills and encourage children?

Are you wanting to be your child's friend, shying away from taking responsibility of correcting your child?

Are you letting your children rule your life?

Do you need parenting skills?

Are you a proud parent?

Are you a good judge of others?

Are you a protector?

Are you being a coward when you should stand and be strong?

Are you very protective over your partner?

Are you being protective of young family members?

Do you get in fights?

Do you fight for family and friends?

Are you putting your life at risk for others?

Do you need witness protection?

Do you need a safe house?

Have you had a summons?

Are you on jury service?

Are you scary if you don't get your own way?

Do people feel the powerful presence of you?

Are you a big meat eater?

Do you have a den?

Do you love roaming free?

Do you insist on doing your own thing?

Are you doing too much?

Are you ruling the nest at home?

Is your behaviour affecting everybody in your home?

Is the atmosphere in your house like a pressure cooker?

Are you on the wild side? Or are you as tame as a Lion?

Are you territorial?

Step into your power.

THE POWER IS NOW

There's great strength in silence.

Do you feel like royalty?

Do you feel like a king or queen?

Have you just got engaged?

Are you planning your wedding?

Do you like safari holidays? Or would you like to go on one?

Are you a prowler?

Have you applied for a big job?

Are you a head hunter?

Are you vain?

Have you got lovely thick hair?

Are you wise?

Possible Life Paths?

Judge, Head of Department, Head Teacher, Head Hunter, Banker, Politician, Entrepreneur.

Firearms Officer, Hair Stylist, Magistrate, Health Visitor, Parenting Advisor, Nursery Nurse.

Marketing, Sales, Blue Chip Companies, Ministry of Defence, Youth justice board, Social Services, NHS, Dentistry.

Any Big Wig job!

Magpie

Magpies are attracted to sparkly and glittery items.

They are striking in appearance, scream and cackle when they don't receive what they want.

Sometimes they can bully other birds.

Are you being anti-social or annoying?

Do you crave things?

Are you a hoarder?

Are you collecting too much stuff?

Are you putting material things before your happiness?

Do you like antiques and sparkly things?

Are you trying to comfort yourself with pretty things?

Are you easily distracted?

Are you restless?

Are you acting suspiciously?

Is your behaviour dodgy or shifty?

Are you stealing things that don't belong to you?

Are you a victim of crime?

Are you having temper tantrums?

Are you an attention seeker?

Are you feeling out of balance?

Are you off balance?

Do you have leg or hip trouble?

Are you going off track?

Are you a copycat?

Are you strutting around?

Are you picking on someone weaker than yourself?

Have you been manipulated or are you being manipulative?

Are you loud and love bickering or arguing for the sake of it?

Are you being outrageously rude and aggressive?

Who's rattled your cage?

Are you a jail bird?

Are you in denial?

Are you looking at both sides of the picture?

Are you taking sides with someone?

Are you being two faced?

Are you a bigot?

Are you caught up in squabbles?

Are you part of a gang?

Does your social media profile match who you really are?

Do you have the proper qualifications?

Are you making sure you check out the credentials of others?

Are your testimonials genuine?

Are people picking on you?

Are you at everyone's beck and call?

Are you having trouble communicating or expressing yourself?

Are you sharing?

Are you bogged down by junk?

Does your house need a good tidy up?

Do you need to hold a garage or car boot sale?

Do you need to go to a charity shop and donate all those items you don't need?

Out with the old in with the new, so get rid of that clutter and brighten up your life.

Are you a bargain hunter?

Do you love a bargain and enjoy looking in second hand shops?

Do you like going to car boot sales?

Are you in a one sided relationship?

Is someone taking advantage of you?

Is their dark side consuming you?

Is someone taking you away from the light?

Do you need a relationship that is much more in balance with your true nature?

Are you making bad choices? There's always more than one choice.

Are you drawn to the bad boys?

Are you afraid of your dark thoughts?

Are you being superstitious?

Are you on the dark side?

Are you surrounded by a dark force?

Sometimes we get drawn to the dark side, because of a hormone imbalance, such as dopamine.

Are you being a dope?

Are you smoking dope?

Are you under an influence?

Are you seeking cheap thrills? Then feeling the shame or guilt?

Are you drawing the wrong attention?

Are you confusing love with lust?

Are you putting yourself in danger?

Are you addicted to the internet?

Are you addicted to gaming?

Are you addicted to texting?

Do you feel exposed?

Are you todays headline?

If your secretive side was exposed, how would you feel?

Has someone got something on you?

Are you being blackmailed?

Are you paying the price for nice things?

Are you selling your soul?

Are you normally balanced but feel suicidal?

Are you spiraling out of control?

Are you having fun at the expense of others?

Is your throat ok? Join a choir or learn to sing.

Is it time to work with others to achieve better results?

Are you being too pushy and over powering on your way to the top. Be careful those same people you push passed will still be there on your way down!

Are you in a job of great responsibility?

Are you a workaholic?

Are you working around the clock?

Are you risking your career with your personal activities?

Are you sharing a business opportunity and helping others to succeed as well?

Are you an opportunist? Spotting any deals?

Bring in the abundance, create new expressions and new ideas.

Have you been rowing with your friends or family?

Are you picking on your partner or a family member?

Has speaking your truth got you into trouble?

Do you believe in freedom of speech?

Do you question your sexuality?

Are you in a one sided love affair?

Are you surrounded by family and friends but you have a deep, inner loneliness?

Would you like more friends?

Have you got **bright light fever**?

Possible Life Paths:

Actor, Singer, Dancer, Model, Car Salesperson.

Politician, Footballer, Jeweler, Banker, Circus Entertainer, Builder.

Construction Worker, Sales & Marketing Representatives, Team Player, Drug Dealer.

Gang Member, Anyone in the limelight.

Mole

A small but very destructive little creature, that loves causing trouble.

Feared mostly by the golf course grounds man!

Do you feel a hole in your life?

Is your life destructive?

Are you burying your head, not facing up to things?

Are your actions destroying other people's work, efforts and lives?

Are you getting on people's nerves?

Are you making a mountain out of a mole hill?

Are you listening into things and then causing trouble?

Are you a secret mole?

Are you planning destruction?

Are you using underhanded tactics?

Are you involved in espionage?

Are you untrustworthy, dishonest, not what you seem?

Are your actions going to effect the less fortunate?

Are you taking any back handers and doing dodgy deals?

Are you involved in money laundering and corruption?

Have you made your money and success at the expense of other's unfortunate circumstances, addictions or desperation?

Have you offered people a new life and reduced them to deprivation?

Have you promised people a safe passage way to a new life in a new country, when really you're a cold hearted con and deceitful person?

Are you deliberately out to con and deceive people?

Are you digging holes where ever you go?

Are you up to no good?

Are you sneaking around?

Are you rushing in like a blind fool?

Is your behaviour like a mole?

Do you probe until you get to the bottom of things?

Do people not see the real you?

Are you really down to earth?

Do people really dig you?

Do you believe what's written in the media or on the news? Or do you make your own mind up?

Do you like conspiracy theories?

Are you what you seem?

Are you deceiving others?

Are you out to cause trouble?

Are you being destructive?

Are you digging up the dirt on some innocent person?

Is your motive to bring someone down?

Are you blackening someone's name?

Are you a spy?

Are you involved in the underworld?

Are you an undercover cop?

Are you bringing someone to justice?

Are you going undercover?

Are you giving out false information?

Are you pretending to be someone you're not?

Do you believe your own lies?

Are you breaking confidentiality?

Are you crossing boundaries?

Are you black mailing someone?

Are you threatening to share information that would have a devastating effect on others?

Are you being paid to be quiet?

Do you have a special mission to carry out?

Are you a spin doctor?

Are you a whistle blower?

Do others trust you when really you are a ruthless cut throat?

Is a situation and truth about to be exposed?

Are you running to hide?

Whatever you're trying to cover up, will one day come to the surface.

Go with your gut, if you know you're on to something keep going.

Are you living a double life?

Are you popping up all over the place?

Do you have obstacles in your life stopping you moving forward?

Are you blind to a situation?

Do you feel in the dark?

Are you totally in the dark?

Are you being deluded?

Are you not seeing what the situation is?

Can you not see through the illusion?

Are you in danger?

Do you need to look for the light?

Can you see a glimmer of light?

Are you digging yourself into an even bigger hole?

Are you able to dig yourself out of trouble?

Do you need to search for the truth?

Do you need to lighten up?

Are you seeking enlightenment?

Have you buried your feelings?

Have you gone underground?

Have you lost your way?

Are you a workaholic?

Are you digging yourself into an early grave?

Have you buried something?

Have you dug something up?

Are you paying your taxes?

Are you being investigated?

Are you under surveillance?

Have you a secret or something to hide?

Are you secretive?

Is your partners past coming to light?

Do you wish to know more about your partners past?

Has somebody caused a hole in your heart or soul?

Do you have a deep secret that you cannot share with anyone?

Have you witnessed an act of violence and aggression that haunts you?

Do you sense a huge injustice in life?

Do you feel you're in a dark tunnel?

Do you like exploration?

Do you enjoy metal detecting?

Do you like digging up relics and history?

Are you digging up the past?

Do you like archeology?

Are you a historian?

Are you digging for treasure?

Do you have a fascination with science?

Is your sense of touch increasing?

Do you need your eyes testing?

Do you have a long term eye problem?

Do you need to keep your eyes on a situation?

Do you have any moles or skin abnormalities?

Do you need sun protection?

Are you drinking enough water?

Are you a keen golfer?

Do you have mud on your face?

Possible Life Paths?

Fracking, Water Diving, Archeologist, Digger, Laborer, Landscaper, Gardener, Grounds Man.

Miner, Gas or Oil Worker, Man Hole Inspector, Maintenance Worker, Drain Specialist.

Ear, Nose, Throat Specialist, Forensic Scientist, DNA Specialist, Taxi Driver, Pipe Fitter.

Undercover Reporter, Paparazzi, Basement Maintenance Worker, Pot Hole Worker, Euro Tunnel Worker.

Security Guard, Surveillance, Detective, Witness Protection, Emergency Services.

Red Cross, Aid Worker, Historian, Archives Record Holder, Problem Solver, Tax Investigator.

Moth

A delicate flying insect who loves nibbling away at your fine items.

Moths are drawn to the light, then get scorched.

Are you nocturnal?

Are you like a butterfly but love night life?

Are you attracting the dark?

Are you struggling?

Are you feeling fragile?

Are you getting more sensitive?

Are you hiding?

Are you engaging in secret night time activities?

Are you full of wisdom?

Are you taking risks?

Are you going to places where you might get injured or hurt?

Have you a deep understanding of life. Inner knowing is natural to you.

Do your inner senses guide you on a daily basis?

Is high intuition a natural part of your path in life?

Do you naturally know where you're going?

Are you disguising and hiding your true emotions and feelings from others?

Are you keeping away from friends and family, because you want to hide?

Have you just experienced pain and sorrow?

Have you just split up with your partner?

Are you about to get burnt?

Is somebody out to swat you?

Are you vulnerable and cannot defend yourself?

Are you being naïve?

Are you struggling in the day?

Is night time lonely?

Do you feel alone?

Do you feel in a dark place?

Are you facing problems on your own?

Do you like your own company at the moment?

Are you withdrawing from your friends?

Are you in recovery?

Are you dancing on your own?

Do you want to come out?

Are you flitting from one project to another?

Are you being indecisive?

Do you have an eating disorder?

Is the reality of life too sensitive for you?

Do you feel safer at night?

Is night time a quiet, sacred space for you?

Do you prefer the silence and peacefulness of the night?

Are you shy?

Are you reserved?

Do you withdraw into a world of your own?

Is life a fantasy to you?

Do you live in your own world?

Are you distracting yourself from the real world?

Are your habits unsociable?

Does your behavior affect others around you?

Do you feel persecuted?

Do you feel you can do no right in the eyes of others?

Do you never feel good enough?

Do you not feel worthy?

Do you have low self-esteem?

Are you a victim?

Do you see your glass as half empty?

Do you expect negative outcomes?

Do you set yourself up to fail?

Do you feel bitterness, sadness, anger and resentment?

Is no matter what you do, never good enough?

Are you seeking the approval and recognition of others?

Has this made you a people pleaser?

Everyone is entitled to self-worth. Turning your negative mind set into a positive one will attract positive outcomes.

Use positive affirmations, the Law of Attraction to build and strengthen your self-esteem and awareness.

Possible Life Paths?

Adult Dancer, Shift Worker, Shelf Filler, Call Center Representative, Taxi Driver.

Garage Attendant, Convenience Store Manager. Fireman, Paramedic, Night

Porter, Fast Food Worker, Pizza Delivery.

Mouse

The mouse lives indoors or outdoors.

A mouse can adapt and live anywhere.

It is a little furry creature with the ability to frighten an elephant.

The mouse is an opportunist, cute but sometimes destructive.

The mouse is very family orientated and quite shy when spotted.

Are you taking advantage and taking things that don't belong to you?

Are you always borrowing things and not returning them?

Are you a pest?

Do you like causing trouble?

Are you a gossip?

Do you repeat what others say, then add to it?

Do you exaggerate the truth?

Are you turning small problems into bigger ones?

Are you forcing entry?

Are you dozy as a door mouse?

Are you poor as a church mouse?

Are you cute?

Do you pay too much attention to detail?

Are you brave in situations?

Are you shy?

Do you run away from situations?

Are you easily intimidated?

Are you nervous?

Is a trap being laid for you?

Are you damaging other people's property?

Are you a squatter?

Do you have an unwelcomed visitor or guest?

Is someone setting a trap to catch you out?

Are you not paying your way?

Are you homeless?

Are you looking for a new home?

Is your presence scary?

Do you make people scream?

Are you part of a gang or group that causes devastation?

Keep an eye on who you circulate with.

Do you get embarrassed or go red easily?

Do your nerves get the better of you at the thought of public speaking?

Are you rushing around, full of nervous tension and anxiety?

Are you taking on too many projects?

Are you being taken advantage of?

Are you stealing other people's ideas & dreams?

Are you gnawing away at others?

Is your destructive behaviour damaging others?

Is what others see the real you?

Are you feeling small? Everybody is entitled to be heard.

Physically are you taking on more than you can handle?

You've only got one heart, look after yours.

Pay attention to your diet, watch what you eat.

Do you pay attention to your personal hygiene?

Are you taking precautions, beware of disease?

Have you got any rashes that need medical attention?

Is your chaotic lifestyle affecting your health?

Maybe it's time for a holiday or small break?

Are you trying for a family? Do you crave a new family?

Have you got more than one family to support?

Are you thinking of fostering or adopting?

Are you being unfaithful?

Have you been leading a double life?

Are your activities affecting others?

Do you have more than one home?

Are you leaving a trail of destruction?

Do you find it hard to stay in one place?

Is it time to move on?

Are you always on the move?

Do you have a phobia?

Possible Life Paths?

Journalist, Paparazzi, Private Investigator,

Taxman, Examiner, Travel Agent, Estate Agent, Midwife, Nurse.

Owl

The owl is the most recognized nocturnal bird and renowned for being full of knowledge and wisdom.

The owl observes all of its surroundings.

Have you just gained a degree?

Are you a wise owl?

Have you got loads of inner knowledge and wisdom?

Have you got good instinct?

Do you know you're a wise soul?

Are you drawn to Egyptology?

Do you want to travel?

Are you beautiful to look at?

Are you a hunter?

Twit Twoo! Are you calling your mate?

Are you wooing someone?

Have you secretly got your eye on someone?

Do you have a secret crush?

Are you learning another language?

Do you always do the right thing?

Do people seek your advice?

Do you like giving advice?

Are you a good judge of others?

Are you good at weighing up situations?

Does becoming a teacher excite you?

Are you a Head Teacher?

Are you a Headhunter?

Are you a head of your department?

Are you a Doctor or PhD?

Are you a deep thinker?

Are you ahead of your time?

Are you a truth seeker?

Do you see yourself as a bit of a scribe? Is it time to write your own novel.

Can you see clearly other people's views?

Can you see through deception?

Are you seeking justice or a solution to a situation?

Are you a policeman that catches the thief in the middle of the night?

Do you have a great sense of your whereabouts and surroundings?

Are you an observer?

Do you teach and help people gain their qualifications?

Are you an instructor or examinations officer?

Do you give lectures on your specialist topic?

Are you an expert and if so, do you share your expertise?

Are you sharing knowledge?

Are you expanding your knowledge?

Are you studying ancient knowledge?

Be careful who you share your knowledge with.

With great knowledge comes great responsibility.

Share it wisely as knowledge in the wrong hands can prove dangerous.

Do you tune into situations and are aware at all times.

Are you astute?

Are you naturally a brain boffin?

Are you interested in the mystery of life?

Do you have an inner knowing?

Are you self-aware?

Do you like studying Egyptology?

Have you thought about going to University?

Have you just passed a degree?

Are you a scholar?

Have you won a scholarship?

Have you just been recognized or won an award for your hard work?

Have you thought about doing an apprenticeship?

Would you like to study medicine, science or mathematics?

Is your studying really take off?

Do you want to retire?

Do people seek your good and fair advice?

Do you work in a court?

Have you got to go to court?

Have you been asked to do jury service?

Have you just been fined?

Are you a good judge of character?

Are you a pillar of society?

Keep a watchful eye.

Don't miss a trick!

Would you like to live in a barn conversion?

Do you like the moon?

Do you like long grass?

Do you like the rain?

Owls don't hunt in the rain.

Have you taken an oath of honour, truth and integrity?

Do you have a flawless character?

Possible Life Paths:

Museum Worker, Head Teacher, Head Hunter, Historian.

Archaeologist, Lecturer, Judge, Barrister, Professor, Librarian.

Examiner, Policeman, Detective, Forensic Scientist.

Doctor, Social Worker, Accountant, Book Keeper, Clerk, Academic.

Night Shift Worker, Security Officer, Arbitrator, Auditor.

Peacock

A truly beautiful bird who likes to strut and show off his beautiful appearance for all to see and adore.

Peacock's can bring out change and transformation. Colour therapy is very beneficial, also drama or dance classes.

The Peacock is about life's ever changing cycles?

The Peacock is an attention seeker and a true showman.

Are you a painter or an artist?

Do you go on stage and perform?

Do you like an audience of admirers?

Do you have your own entourage?

Are you an actor or an actress?

Are you a show off?

Are you a poser?

Are you puffing yourself out?

Do you know you are very attractive?

Do you have magnetism and charisma?

Are you a holiday rep or are you in the entertainment industry?

Are you the star of the show? Lucky you!

Are you vain?

Do you love yourself?

Are you in love with love?

Do you enjoy the finer things in life?
Splendid surroundings, good food, wine and grandeur.

Are you being vain?

Do you want that attention?

Are you the center of attention?

Do you feel all eyes are on you?

Is status everything to you?

Do you feel the centre of the universe?

Are you a creature of beauty?

Have you got everything, the looks and walk, that comes at a price?

Are you happy surrounded by your materialism?

Do you lose friends because they feel inadequate to you?

Do you take too long to get ready so you miss out on normal everyday life?

Are you so attention seeking that you are hard work to have as a friend?

Are you obsessed with the beauty industry, spending too much money on it?

Are you not accepting of age and unhappy with your looks?

Have you accepted yourself as you truly are?

Are you wearing a mask?

Are you a celebrity or important in your circle of friends and family?

Do people adore you?

Are you a stalker?

Do you adore your celebrities?

Are you obsessed, wanting to know their every move?

Do you demand attention?

What vibe are you sending out?

Be careful what you ask for.

You can attract the wrong partner if you stand out too much.

There's always someone younger than you. Be happy in your own skin.

Are people envious or jealous of you?

Are you jealous or envious of others?

Do people want to be you?

Do you have amazing vision and attention to detail?

Are you smart and don't miss a trick?

Can you see what others miss?

Eyes are the windows to your soul.

Do you have an appreciation of the arts?

Do you like graffiti?

Have you just had a tattoo?

Do you like body art or piercings?

Do you like have your nails done?

Are you thinking about changing your appearance?

Do you spend a fortune on designer clothes?

Do you dress to impress?

Do you love dancing?

Would you like to learn to dance?

Do you need healing?

Would you like to travel to India?

Are you psychic?

Are you under psychic attack?

Peacock teaches us all about life, death, and rebirth. Sometimes the old has to be replaced with the new.

Have you just lost a loved one?

Are you celebrating a pregnancy or birth?

Have you had a profound spiritual experience?

Is your third eye awakening?

Have you been enlightened?

Do you feel you're the phoenix rising out of the flames of the fire?

Transformation is happening. Out with the old and in with the new.

Possible Life Paths?

Hairdresser, Beautician, Nail Technician, Spa Therapist, Plastic Surgeon.

Make Up or Tattoo Artist, Face Painter. Entertainer, Comedian, Talent Spotter,

Singer, Pop Star, Reality TV, Host, Holiday Rep. Body Building,

Pheasant

The pheasant is striking in its appearance.

The pheasants like woodlands, hedges and lay seven or fifteen eggs.

Are seven or fifteen lucky for you?

Do you think you might be getting the seven-year itch?

Seven can be about new cycles of change.

Sometimes people can get very jealous of beautiful things.

Do you get jealous?

Is someone jealous of you?

Are you a player?

Are you a gamer?

Are you playing games?

Are you up for a challenge?

Are you checking out the competition around you?

Are you living in a fantasy dream world?

Are you putting others at risk?

Is gambling getting you into trouble?

Are you playing Russian Roulette and gambling your life away?

Is your habit needing some professional help?

Do you know someone who owns a gun?

Do you know anyone hiding any weapons?

Is this putting you at risk or in possible danger?

Some people enjoy a chase, are you playing the game?

Are you sweet and beautiful?

Are you naive?

Are you gentle?

Are you getting a bit of an easy reputation?

Are you a victim of domestic violence?

Do you want to leave your present partner but fear the consequences?

Has someone been cruel to you?

Are you surrounded by violence and aggression?

Have you seen violence and horrible things?

Are you in danger?

Have you been beaten or abused?

Are you too weak to stand up for yourself?

Do you feel like giving up?

Are others hunting you down?

Do you feel like somebody's meat?

Are you being chased?

Are you hiding?

Are you lying low?

Has life left you battered and worn out?

Do you feel numb and dead inside?

Is violence all you know?

Do you shoot things as a hobby?

Are you a gangster?

Are you the good or bad cop?

Are you seeking a more simplistic way of life?

Possible Life Paths?

Domestic Violence Officer, Help line Worker, Women's Refuge Helper.

Conservation Worker, Game Keeper, Grounds Man, Child Protection Team,

Social Worker, Carer, Aid Worker, Casualty Nurse.

Policeman, Fire Arms Officer.

Rabbit

The rabbit is a fast moving character that can freeze like a statue under a spotlight or when in danger.

Don't make any drastic decisions, freeze like a rabbit and think things through.

Wait until you are out of danger before you think about movement.

Are you taking good care of yourself?

Be gentle with yourself and withdraw from crowds and noise.

Do you look gentle but could be vicious?

Is someone trying to give you cuddles but you want to break free?

Have you scratched someone lately?

Do people see you as a pest?

Are you hopping mad?

Are you being hunted?

Are you scared?

Do you freeze when you're frightened?

Are you hiding?

Are you burying your head?

Do you feel trapped?

Are you full of fear?

Are you feeling vulnerable?

Are you worried and anxious?

Are you shy and timid?

Are you being weedy or needy?

Are you quiet and reserved?

Do you find life harsh and brutal?

Springtime is very lucky for you, when you will be at your most fertile time!

Are you feeling lucky?

Are you really fertile?

Are you pregnant?

There could be news of a pregnancy but be careful. Babies are great if the pregnancy is planned.

Do you want to start a family?

Do you want lots of children?

Do you love your family?

Do you want to be a foster parent?

Do you enjoy the company of others?

Are you really social?

Do you like large gatherings?

Do you like nature?

Are you aware of your environment?

Have you got great awareness?

Are you hopping forward in leaps and bounds?

Do you love freedom?

Are you an early riser?

Do you have trouble with your teeth?

Do you have a disease?

Have you caught a disease?

Are you infectious?

Do you have a rash?

Have you just caught something?

Are you contagious?

Have you just been quarantined?

Are you spreading your germs?

Possible Life Paths?

Plumber, Construction Worker, Social Worker,
Family Advisor,
Health Visitor.

Festival Organizer, Community Organizer,
Outdoor Activities Trainer.

Nursery Nurse, Dentist, Dental Nurse,
Orthodontist, Midwife, Family Planning.

Rat

Rats spread disease, love hiding out in sewers and stagnant places.

Is your life dark and dingy?

Are you being a rat?

Do you have a dismal and bleak outlook on life?

Are you aware of undercurrents of negativity in society?

Are you spreading negativity?

Negativity can spread! Stay away from anything that can contaminate you!

Are you spreading disease?

Are you being hygienic?

Do you need a health check?

Have you had your inoculations?

Have you got a rash?

Do you feel unwell?

Is your drinking water fresh?

Is it time to have a good clean up?

Get out of the sewer and clean up your life!

Don't neglect yourself, shower and be clean.

Is something nasty around you?

Are you being used and abused?

Are you scary to others?

Are you gnawing away at someone?

Have you got your teeth into someone?

Are you attacking someone?

Are you being vicious and attacking for no reason?

Do you have a nasty and vindictive mind?

Are you being malicious?

Do you make people scream or cry?

Do you feel shame or guilt about something?

Are you deceiving people?

Are you being secretive about your habits?

Have you a dark side or secret?

Are you hiding something?

Are you covering up your tracks?

Are you spreading rumours?

Are you involved in spreading propaganda?

Are you a whistle blower?

Are you using someone for your own gratification?

Are you taking advantage of others?

Time to scurry away from those incestuous relationships?

Scuttle away from those mind control groups.

Stay away from exploitation and modern slavery.

Are you being faithful?

Are you being honest in your relationships?

Are you living with a rat?

Are you a cheat?

Are you a love rat?

Are you leading a double life?

Do you have a trail of children behind you?

Are you overcrowded in your living space?

Are you living next door to a rat?

Are you protecting yourself in work?

Are you a fly tipper?

One man's rubbish is another man's treasure!

Are you messy and disorganized?

Lighten up and change something in your life!

Maybe it's time to clean up and redecorate!

Choose bright colours for your clothes!

Are you resourceful?

Are you a survivor?

Are you rat-assed?

Love yourself and know your true worth!

Possible Life Paths?

Pest Control, Plumber, Newspaper Reporter, Paparazzi, Government Officials.

Agencies, Politicians, Private Investigator, Journalists.

Hygienist, Dentist, Refuse Collector, Cleaner, Drain Cleaner.

Robin

The Robin is a small bird, who's very strong willed.

They are very determined and have great inner strength

The Robin is very territorial and lays five to six eggs.

Are the numbers five or six lucky for you?

Are you puffing yourself up?

The Robin defends his own territory and gets into fights over what he thinks is his!

Are you being reminded of a strong family member?

The presence of a Robin could mean a deceased family member is reminding you to stay strong.

Do you have no family?

Do you feel lonely?

Are you Billy no mates?

Do you prefer being in your own company?

Do you feel lost and don't fit in?

Better to stand alone than be in the wrong company.

Is someone winding you up?

Do you see red?

Are you angry?

Anger needs to be dealt with or you could end up on your own.

Do you need anger management or counselling?

Remember the **Traffic lights**.

● RED – STOP – Are you angry/cross? Are things not going your way?

● AMBER- THINK- Do not say or do anything.

● GREEN – GO GET HELP - Stay calm, breathe back into control. (Cause & Effect)

Maybe it's time to release any anger and bitterness?

Are you territorial?

Are you trustworthy?

Are you loyal?

Are you big-ing yourself up?

Are you small but have a big presence?

Are you small but extremely strong?

Do you need to stand your ground or back down?

Are you a strong character?

Is it time to stand on your own two feet?

Do you stand strong?

Have you an inner strength?

Start believing in yourself. Find your own inner strength.

Are you learning to be independent & self-reliant?
Are you a survivor?

Do you spend a lot of time thinking about sex?

The colour red symbolizes power, that draws attention to you.

Have you been sexually abused?

Do you feel you've been used and abused?

Do you feel you've been taken advantage?

Have you just been dumped?

Is someone around you very angry?

Are you controlling or being controlled?

Are you thinking about your family all the time?

Do you fight for your family?

Is your family everything to you?

Are you having to stand strong for your family?

Do your family turn to you for strength and direction?

Do you have family problems and arguments at home?

Do your actions affect your partner or children?

Are you cutting yourself off from friends and family?

Do you have angry neighbours?

Do you feel raw?

Is it time to let go of painful issues?

Are you experiencing rejection?

Are you withdrawing from the world?

Are you physically over doing it?

Are you putting on weight?

Do you need to watch your weight?

Keep an eye on your blood pressure.

Don't ignore your health!

Do you have a sore throat?

Do you have chest problems?

Do you like winter?

Are you spending a lot of time thinking about winter?

Do you have a profound connection to nature?

Do you have the complete balance between the material and spiritual?

Do you accept the cycles of life?

Do you love your garden?

Are you a keen gardener?

Do you love nature?

Possible Life Paths?

Bank Manager, Journalist, Spy, Soldier, Armed Forces.

Manager, Policeman, Lawyer, Student, Social Worker.

Health Visitor, Gardener, Farmer, Self Employed.

Entrepreneur, Troubleshooter.

Seagull

The Seagull is a very large, noisy and intimidating bird.

Are you a bit of a chancer?

Are you an opportunist?

Are you quick at making decisions?

Are you quick off the mark?

Are you always at the beginning of opportunities that have just taken off?

Are you a financial investor?

Do you see yourself as an entrepreneur?

Is this a good time to start a business?

Are you trying to be self-sufficient?

Are you mindful of your actions towards the environment?

Are you environmentally friendly?

Do you use biodegradable products?

Do you see yourself as an ecowarrior?

Are you conscious of global warming?

Are you aware of your own carbon footprint?

Do you have concerns for the next generation on our planet?

Do you love your planet?

Do you believe in World Peace?

Are you a bit of a hippy?

Are you an activist?

Is it time to start a campaign?

Are you a conservationist?

Do you hate pesticides and chemicals?

Are you just a litterbug?

Do you need to recycle?

Do you need to go to the tip?

Do you need to empty your garage or spare room of junk?

Do you need to go to the seaside for a break?

Do you like the sea?

Do you want to go on a cruise?

Do you want to be a Fisherman?

Do you pick up others rubbish?

Are you always cleaning up after other people?

Do you feel someone is about to crap on you?

Are you fed up of cleaning and feel your worth more?

Are you using a food bank?

Are you stealing and snatching food?

Is it time to add organic food to your diet?

Is it time to meditate and listen to music?

Is it time for vibrational medicine?

Possible Life Paths?

Cleaner, Refuge Collector, Road Sweeper, Litter Picker, Boat Yard Worker.

Antique Dealer, Second Hand Car Dealer, Fisherman, Lumberjack, Carpenter,

Compost Maker, Immigration Control.

Entrepreneur, Renewable Energy, Organic Gardner, Activist.

Aid Worker, Fair Trade Operator. Conservationist, Campaigner.

Sheep

The sheep is a lovely woolly coated animal that bleats, plays and has a very gentle nature.

Is there gentleness about you?

Are you meek and mild?

Are you full of kindness and compassion?

Do you have a sweet personality?

Are you a peacemaker?

Do you like socializing?

Are you feeling sheepish?

Are you playing follow the leader?

Are you a copycat?

Do you do what others tell you?

Have you no mind of your own?

Do you carry on regardless of your own thoughts?

Have you lost your identity?

Are you following in others footsteps?

Do you not want to think what you're doing?

Do you have the same routine day in and day out?

Do you want a change of routine?

Are you following the latest trends?

Do you own the same technology as everyone else?

Do you feel insignificant?

Do you fit in?

Do you feel the odd one out?

Do you feel left out in the cold?

Has the warmth gone from your heart?

Are you weak?

Do you just agree with people?

Are you a people pleaser?

Do you sit on the fence worrying that your view will upset others?

Can you be a bit indecisive?

Are you bleating and moaning all the time?

Do you feel bored?

Are you being treated fairly?

Do you feel like someone's meat?

Are you like a lamb to the slaughter?

Is someone being rough with you?

Are people taking advantage of your kind way?

Are you innocent?

Are you ignorant to the pain and suffering of others?

Do others flock around you?

Are you part of a peaceful organisation?

Is someone trying to silence you?

Do you need a body guard?

Do you need someone to watch over you?

Is someone watching you?

Is someone tracking your movements?

Is your mum the absolute best?

Do you have a special bond with your mum?

Do you have a huge family?

Are you looking at starting a family?

Do you miss your family?

Have you lost a member of your family?

Do you feel like a lost sheep or are you the black sheep of the family?

Are you different to other family members?

Do you want a DNA test?

Do you need a haircut?

Are you having any problems with your feet?

Do you have any problems with your mouth?

Do you like cuddling and hugging?

Are you always warm?

Do you like warm winter coats?

Are you a great shepherd looking after your flock?

Do you like chasing around?

Are you a lost soul?

Are you the leader?

Do you love spring?

Do you spring forward in spring?

Possible Life Paths?

Rescue Worker, Help Line Advisor, Domestic Violence Officer.

Children's Nanny or Nurse, Child Minder, Baby Sitter, Midwife, Pediatrician.

Rug Maker, Carpet Layer, Chef, Shepherd, Farmer.

Slug

The slug has a very sticky and slimy body and usually comes out after heavy rain.

The slug eats and gnaws away at greenery, leaving a trail behind them.

Do your habits irritate others?

Are you leaving a trail of destruction behind you?

Are you winding people up, making them angry?

Do you like stopping people from achieving their outcome?

Are you slow or are your actions slowing other people up?

Are you holding people up?

Are people waiting too long for replies to emails they have sent to you or calls they have made to you?

Try not to be late and keep people waiting as this can have a knock on effect.

Are you a pest, do people not like you?

Are you a slimy person, is your company not welcome?

Are you wrecking what other people have worked hard to achieve?

Have you shown your true colours?

Are you jealous of people?

Are you wiping out other people's ideas?

Are you irritating and annoying?

Do you never finish anything?

Finish one job properly and then start the next.

Are people trying to kill you?

Are people trying to track you down?

Are you feeling a little sluggish?

Are you overeating and indulging?

Are you obese?

Do you have a sluggish immune system?

Are you trashing your environment?

Do you always find yourself in sticky situations?

Have you been made redundant?

Do you feel redundant?

Do you fear redundancy?

Possible Life Paths?

Casual Worker, Gardener, Demolition, Nutritionist, Bailiff.

Credit Agencies, Private Investigator, Debt Collector, Dietician.

Health Care Assistant.

Snail

The snail is a slow mover and never in a hurry.

Do you find other people are rushing past you?

Are you feeling left behind by everybody zooming forward in their life?

Do you find that life is too fast for you?

Do you suffer from neck, shoulder or back problems?

Do you carry all your troubles on your back?

Do you carry the world's problems on your back?

Have you got no back bone?

Are you telling the same old story?

Is your past catching up with you?

Are you always on the move?

Do you keep moving house?

Are you homeless?

Are you restless and can't seem to settle down in one place or job?

Do you never settle in a place long enough to call it your home?

Is someone after you, forcing you to move on?

Has someone wrecked your house?

Is someone trying to stamp on you?

Is someone trying to poison you?

Are you leaving a trail of devastation and destruction behind you?

Are you slimy?

Do you envy others?

Have you got a hard shell?

Do you act hard?

Have you just been crushed?

What are you eating away at?

What's getting to you?

What are you hiding from?

Come out and show your true self. Show your true colours.

Are you working at a snail's pace?

Are you a slow learner?

Have you got dyslexia?

Do you not pick things up as quickly as other people?

Are others irritated by your snail's pace?

Are you worried about old age?

Are you slowing down because of your age?

Is life passing you by?

Do you need more vegetables in your diet?

Do you need healing?

Have you thought of Yoga, Pilates or Tai Chi?

Do you like the rain?

Possible Life Paths?

Supermarket Attendant, Bag Filler, Removals, Delivery Men, Bus Driver. Fast Food.

Spider

Works very hard making an amazing construction and intricate network of webs.

Are you a workaholic?

Is your work intricate?

Are you trapping someone in a web of deceit?

Are you part of a group that is weaving and deceiving?

Are you or the group you hang around with, terrorizing and frightening others?

Are you constructing a trap to catch others?

Do you try to prevent others from going forward?

Are you out to catch people out?

Is your presence scary?

Are you creepy?

Do you give people the shivers?

Are you creeping around?

Are you a predator?

Does your presence arouse fear in other people?

Are people afraid of you?

Are your activities on the dark side?

Are you someone who's involved in a network of criminal activity?

Are you about to join a network of darkness?

Beware of internet and phone scams or fraud.

Be careful of your comments on social media.

Do you know someone who takes all the credit for what others do?

Do you feel that all eyes are on you?

Is someone out to spin you a yarn?

Do you feel a victim?

Are you being consumed, drained and devoured by others around you?

Do you know a widow or single person who consumes the energy of other people?

Do you feel there's a negative or dark force after you?

Have you got an unhealthy attachment?

Has someone got an unhealthy attachment to you?

Are you being transparent?

Are you a bull shitter?

Do you love the sound of your own voice?

Are you full of false promises?

Are you hi-tech?

Are you a networker?

Small spiders- Lucky you, small amounts of money may be coming to you.

Big spiders- Can be an Omen, good or bad. Keep an eye on your finances.

Lots of spider webs- beware of networks including on line.

More spiders, so more opportunities, more networking, network yourself, talk to people and spread the word about your business.

Are your plans sustainable?

Have one of your plans or projects fallen through?

Is there a power struggle going on in any of your relationships?

Are you dominant and overpowering in your relationships or is someone dominating you?

Are you being deceitful and dishonest in your relationships?

Are you in a no win situation?

Are you having one night stands?

Have you been stood up?

Has somebody got you dangling on a string?

Are you caught up in a trap?

Is someone out to trap you?

Are you laying a trap?

What is bugging you so much?

Are you making life so hard for yourself?

Is your life out of balance?

Have you just been let down?

If a spider falls, it rescues itself on its lifeline.

Maybe it's time to learn self-reliance?

If at first you don't succeed, try and try again!

A Spider rebuilds his web, even when someone destroys it. Don't give up. Even if someone has ruined your plans, never quit, keep going!

Moving on? Do you need to blow the cobwebs away?

Have you got lots of cobwebs in your house?

If so spiders will always find another place to go, so don't worry about clearing them.

Never kill spiders, they're there to help you eat up those obstacles that are blocking your path to success.

Are you seeing the true picture?

Have you got poor eye sight or double vision?

Do you need to get your eye's tested?

Have you had eye correction surgery?

Are you really seeing what's there?

Do you have an eye for attention to detail?

Have you got trouble with your circulation?

Have you got trouble with walking or any other movement involving your legs?

Do you enjoy physical exercise or activities?

Do you like trampolining?

Could knitting be a stress reliever for you?

Are you a great Parent?

Are you solitary?

Are you always thinking about your next meal?

Have you had a vision?

Are you a visionary?

Possible Life Paths?

Entrepreneur, Project Worker, Policeman, Detective, Judge, Solicitor.

Managing Director, Prison Officer, Planning
Officer, Surveyor.

Sales Representative and Marketing Agent, Pest
Controller, Network Marketer, Help Line
Advisor.

Architect, Seamstress, Website Administrator,
Tourist Guides, Concierge.

Mountain and Rock Climbers, Window Cleaner,
Customer Sales Representative.

Dance Instructor or Student, Electrician,
Plumber, Construction Worker.

Gang Member, Drug Dealer, Terrorist, Football
Hooligan.

Squirrel

Squirrels use their bushy tails for balance as they climb up trees and along branches.

The squirrel has lots of hidey-holes for his winter store of nuts.

This is a great time for all types of communication and networking.

Don't put all your energy into one project just yet.

Be like a squirrel and plan things out.

Out of one small acorn grows a huge oak tree.

This is a great time for important phone calls, signing contracts and attending job interviews.

You're in perfect form, harmony and balance so make the most of this window of golden opportunity.

Swing into action, grab and seize your opportunities!

As one door closes, another one opens with endless opportunities?

This could be the ideal time for interviews and meetings.

Is it a good time for business and commerce proposals?

Or lucrative deals?

It's a good time to ask for a loan or apply for a mortgage.

It's a good time to ask for that promotion or raise in salary!

State your intentions and go for it!

Whatever you are thinking about do it, follow your intuition.

Look for signs of synchronicity, nothings by chance.

Is it time to study the Law of Attraction?

Ask and it will be given.

Put your dreams and aspirations out there.

Are you dynamic?

Are you great at communication?

Are you strong at getting your view across?

Are you signing contracts or important documents?

Are you putting savings into a few schemes?

Are you extremely resourceful?

Are you careful at planning for the future?

Are you good with your finances?

Do you over spend?

Do you buy too much of everything?

Are you good at managing and budgeting your money?

Do you save money for a rainy day?

Do you have lots of hiding places for your money?

Do you have a secret stash of money?

Are you hiding money away from your partner?

Are you storing food?

Are you hoarding and wasteful?

Is your home and work, in or out of balance?

Have you thought of entering or participating in a competition?

Are you competitive?

Have you got a partner that really listens, understands and gets you?

Although the sign of a Squirrel is mostly positive, there is a destructive side.

Are you telling tales?

Beware of false promises and charlatans everywhere.

Have you been let down by a business partner or friend?

Do you know your business partner as well as you should?

Try not to mix business with pleasure and beware of having friends in business.

Are you good at gymnastics?

Do you need to go to the gym?

Is your energy high or low?

Should you be a vegetarian, is life too toxic for you?

Do you need more nuts in your diet?

Are you a bit eccentric or nutty?

Are you a hard nut?

Are you hard on the outside and soft in the center?

Are you cracking up?

Do you like the crack?

Are you up for a laugh?

Possible Life Paths?

Managing Director, Business Development Manager, Entrepreneur.

Public Speaker, Salesman, Negotiator, Host, Function Organizer.

Arbitrator, Recruitment, Advertisers, Wedding & Events Planner, Comedian.

Bank manager, Insurance Advisor, Tax Officer, Investment Broker.

Gymnastics, Circus Entertainer, Paparazzi Reporter.

Swan

Swans are very pure and they only choose one soul mate for a lifetime.

Swans represent purity, peacefulness, faithfulness and honour.

The swan is a lovely, beautiful creature and is a good sign if you've been ill or had an operation.

You will soon recover with the lovely energies of the swan.

Are you pure in your thoughts?

Do you have integrity?

Are you honorable and trustworthy?

Do you have high morals and standards?

Are you looking for a mate to stay with you?

Have you found your true soulmate?

If you have just met somebody, this could be your possible partner for life?

Are you in a relationship where you are both happy and content?

Will you be loving and loyal to one another throughout this lifetime?

Do you both adore one another?

Is your partner the most important thing to you?

Is your partner protective over you?

The Swan makes a great parent but pushes their offspring out into the world at a young age.

The swan is very good at encouraging its children to leave its nest and venture out on their own life purpose.

They are very loyal, but are very strong, with a wing span that can break an arm.

Do you see yourself as a bodyguard?

Would you like to be a bodyguard?

You are highly protected at this time.

A Swan's strength is its love.

When they pair and kiss they turn into a love heart, making people open hearted.

Is your heart center opening?

Swans can promote peace and calm.

This could be a time of emotional healing in your life.

Learn to swim with the sea of emotions of life, go with the flow, don't be a fish out of water.

Do you trust your partner completely?

In unity two become one.

Are you mirroring one another?

Do you have romance on your mind?

Do you live for your partner?

Are you inseparable?

Do you worship and adore your mate?

Do you love romantic nights out?

Are you in love with love?

Are you truly, madly and deeply in love?

Are you choosing a partner for life?

Do you want to be with your partner for life?

Do you want to walk into the sunset together?

Are you starry eyed?

Do you like the twilight?

Do you like watching the sunset and sunrise together?

Have you just got engaged?

Are you getting married?

Are you honest, truthful and loyal?

Do you love lakes?

Do you love peace?

Do you like ballet?

Are you elegant?

Are you clumsy?

Are you stubborn?

Are you clean leaving?

Is your true identity being recognized?

Has it been revealed who you truly are?

Do you spend a lot of your time thinking about revelations?

Are you seeking or reaching enlightenment?

Is your consciousness evolving?

Possible Life Paths?

Any path that is truly pure and spreads unconditional love, peace and compassion to humanity.

Wasp

A feared insect with a sting in its tail, attacking for no reason.

Have you just been stung?

Is someone trying to rip you off?

Is someone close causing trouble?

Are you under attack?

Are you about to get hurt?

Have you been mugged?

Is someone controlling your mind?

Are you a consumer?

Are you influenced by commercialism or advertising?

Beware of Payday Loans and On Line Betting.

Does seeing a Wasp terrify you?

Do you need someone to fight your battle for you?

Is someone expecting you to pay their dinner or drinks bill?

Is someone getting you to pay for them all the time?

Are others taking advantage of your generous nature?

Like the Wasp, are you being vicious and attacking for no reason?

Are you going out of your way to cause trouble?

Has your bad behaviour hurt others?

Are you planning an attack?

Do you enjoy being mean?

Are you enjoying spreading rumours?

Do you like being spiteful?

Do you have a vicious tongue?

Are you being judgmental?

Is there negativity around you?

Are you one that's negative?

Are you buzzing around and annoying others?

Are you irritable?

Do you take your bad moods out on others?

Do you blame everyone else for your bad luck?

Are you trying to swindle or deceive someone?

Are you after someone else's money or property?

Do you pretend to be someone you're not?

Are you a conman or thief?

Are you a non-conformist?

Are you a whistle blower?

Are you ready to swarm into action?

Do you think of joining the forces?

Are you a force not to be messed with?

Do you like yourself?

Are you about to cause huge trouble for yourself?

Do you like your life?

Has someone told you something that has made your ears buzz?

Are you being foolish?

Are you frightened of injections?

Do you have phobias?

Are you spending your time gossiping?

Are you part of the corporate world?

Do you have a sting in your tail?

Possible Life Paths?

Escort, Drug Dealer, Loan Shark, Money Lender, Anesthetist, Dentist.

Arms Dealer, Activist, Whistle Blower, Office Mole, Private Investigator.

Cowboy Builder, Fake Agents, Hackers. Any unscrupulous path.

Wolf

The wolf has a striking appearance and strong presence.

Not only does he have beautiful eyes, but a lovely fur coat.

The wolf is a wonderful powerful hunter and very in tune with its senses.

Wolfs are strongly associated with shamanic teachings.

Are you on a shamanic journey?

Are you on a vision quest?

Are your senses reawakening?

Is your awareness developing?

Is your subconscious coming to full consciousness?

Do you spend your time in meditation, prayer or practicing mindfulness?

Are your dreams trying to tell you something?

Are your dreams reflecting your personal life?

Do you have a special dream?

Does your reoccurring dream haunt you?

Do you love dream catchers or are you thinking of buying one?

Do you enjoy being outdoors?

Are you solitary?

Have you been howling or crying?

Are you a predator?

Are you a stalker?

Are you a scout?

Are you a prowler?

Are you sniffing or creeping around?

Are you keeping track of someone?

Are you out to lure someone into a trap or a false sense of security?

Are you a big bad wolf?

Is your intention to protect or take advantage of an innocent person?

Are you cruel or vicious?

Are you aware of the impact of your negative behaviour on others?

Are you in a gang?

Do you gang up on others?

Don't take risks walking alone, there's great safety and protection in numbers.

Wolves look after each other as a pack.

Are you family orientated?

Are you sharing your new found knowledge with family members?

Is a family secret worrying you?

Are you good at keeping secrets?

Are you surrounded by family secrets?

Are there revelations about your family coming to the surface, that you'd sooner keep secretive and hidden?

Are you being hurt or harmed by your own flesh and blood?

Has your family ripped your heart apart?

Have you been pushed to the limits by your own family?

Are you working through your family's karma?

Is family your one and only weakness?

Are you being exhausted by your family's constant demands?

Do you feel the odd one out of your family?

Do you try and fit in or do you stay true to who you really are?

Have you cut yourself off from your family?

Have you isolated yourself from friends and family?

Give them a call and round them up, communication is the key.

Are you working away from home and missing your family?

Is it time to return home to your family?

Are you fiercely protective over a family member?

Do you know that someone is in the wrong but you still defend them?

Are you covering up someone else's mistake?

Are you in the family business?

Have you achieved success by going through the back door?

Is a family member or friend about to rip you off?

Are you in a family and you feel isolated, the pack doesn't pay you attention and is getting on great without you?

Is their favouritism amongst your family members?

Has your self-esteem been affected by a cruel family members comment?

Stand up for yourself, prove your family members wrong.

Be your true authentic self, not what others want you to be.

You can't be all things to all people.

Family are here to teach us life lessons and sometimes mirror what karma we need to work through.

We are all family, we are all connected, we are all one, we just need to recognise and know this.

Is there sibling rivalry going on your family home?

At this time, you can rely on your family for assistance and support.

Your family will always love you no matter what.

Are you the one who your family turn to for strength and support?

Do people fear your family's presence?

Have your family got a bad reputation?

Do you have a suspicious mind?

Are you wary and cautious when meeting new people?

Are you a good leader?

Are you good at working on your own, but also a team player?

Are you starting out on new adventures?

Do you love the elements and being outdoors?

Are you walking in your ancestor's footprints or trail?

Is your life on the right track?

Have you strayed from your path?

Have you chosen the wrong path in life? Seek positive signs to help you change your direction.

Are you trying to break habits of behaviour?

Do you depend on another for success?

Are you lost or feeling alone?

Don't be frightened to show your emotions, everybody needs to cry. It is not a weakness.

The cry of the wolf returns his pack to him. There is much strength in numbers!

Are you trying to warn others?

Are you baring your teeth, trying to warn someone off?

Get your family to reconnect with outdoor activities or nature.

Be at one with the healing powers of nature.
Take a walk in a forest, breathe in the fresh air.

Do you like family gatherings and feasts?

Is your family always on the move?

Do you like sharing and cooking food for your
family members?

Spend time away from technology, go and look
for your power animal.

You're powerful, step into your power!

Have you just bought a dog?

Are you a great companion?

Are you more productive in a team?

Do you need backup from your team?

Do you need to call on a team or family member
for assistance?

Is your sense of smell and hearing rising?

Are you receiving psychic experiences?

Have you experienced Déjà vu?

Do you have all your basic needs, a roof over
your head, warmth, food and water?

Are you humble and full of gratitude?

Are you a strong survivor?

Are you a pioneer?

Are you someone who's not taken in by materialism?

Are you full of unconditional love?

Maybe you should sponsor a wolf?

Are you intuitive?

Are you a victim of crime?

Have you just been beaten up?

Are you honourable and trustworthy?

Are you reliable and solid as a rock?

Do you have a striking appearance?

Do you have teeth or gum problems?

Are you in the family way?

Are you being promiscuous?

Possible Life Paths?

Armed forces, Police, Social Services, Teachers. Heads of Departments, Managing Director.

Family Liaison, Therapist, Surgeon, Dentist. Butcher, Scout, Arbitration, Marriage Guidance.

Government Worker, Aid Worker, Problem Solver, Troubleshooter.

Surveillance, Private Investigator, Observation, Planning Engineer.

Solicitor, Barrister, Secret Society/Organisation.

Bodyguard, Spiritual Advisor.

Revelations of Feathers

A Feather falling from the sky in front of you, means an immediate connection between you and God\Universe\Cosmos\and All That Is.

This is a Holy Moment in Time, intervention from above, heaven coming to earth.

If you see one White Feather, it's your Angels business or calling card.

Ask your Angel for their help and assistance. Your Angel is aware of your problem and is by your side.

Three White Feathers, this is your Angel trying to warn you or get your full attention about something.

One Black Feather, means a difficult or distressing time is coming to an end.

A very Long Feather means; do you need to keep a journal or perhaps write a novel or play? As this encourages creative writing.

One Owl Feather, means privileged wisdom and knowledge is coming to you.

One Hawk/Eagle Feather means ancestors are close by. Tune in to your ancestral heritage and life path.

A Tiny Feather means fertility or you'll hear news of a pregnancy.

One Large Feather, do you need to cleanse, detox or smudge?

Your Personal Reading

Thank you for reading this book, if you wish to further explore the fascinating revelations from the Animal Kingdom and share your own thoughts and experiences from reading this book?

Please join our growing community and receive a discount on your first personal Animal Reading

www.animalreflections.co.uk

You can also join our group on Facebook.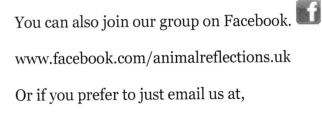

www.facebook.com/animalreflections.uk

Or if you prefer to just email us at,

ask@animalreflections.co.uk

All feedback is welcome!

Jane Giddings, Bristol, September 2016.

62809244R00139

Made in the USA
Charleston, SC
22 October 2016